PREPARING, DESIGNING, LEADING WORKSHOPS &

PREPARING, DESIGNING, LEADING WORKSHOPS

a humanistic approach

Susan Cooper

Cathy Heenan

VNR VAN NOSTRAND REINHOLD COMPANY
NEW YORK   CINCINNATI   TORONTO   LONDON   MELBOURNE

Originally published in 1980 by Cahners Books, Boston.

Copyright © 1980 by Cathy Heenan and Susan Cooper

Library of Congress Catalog Card Number: 83-23601

ISBN: 0-442-21722-6

Manufactured in the United States of America

Published by Van Nostrand Reinhold Publishing
135 West 50th Street, New York, N.Y. 10020

Van Nostrand Reinhold
480 Latrobe Street
Melbourne, Victoria 3000, Australia

Van Nostrand Reinhold Company Limited
Molly Millars Lane
Wokingham, Berkshire, England

Macmillan of Canada
Division of Gage Publishing Limited
164 Commander Boulevard
Agincourt, Ontario M1S 3C7, Canada

15 14 13 12 11 10 9 8 7 6 5 4 3

Library of Congress Cataloging in Publication Data

Cooper, Susan, 1947–
    Preparing, designing & leading workshops.

    1. Forums (Discussion and debate)   2. Leadership.
3. Meetings.   I. Heenan, Cathy, 1945–   II. Title.
III. Title: Preparing, designing, and leading workshops.
LC6519.C66   1984   371.3'7   83-23601
ISBN 0-442-21722-6

Dedication

We dedicate this book to our
husbands, Marc and Bob, who
have supported us in our creative
efforts and have encouraged us to
be all that we are.

Contents

Appendices: Worksheets & Tear-Out Forms 105

Acknowledgment

The material for this book comes from many sources, including the various workshops we have each attended, and from the many skilled leaders/teachers/trainers who have shared their expertise with us. Since it is not possible to thank them all individually, we would like this book to be our way of saying 'thank you' for their help. However, we would like to personally thank Leie Lindman Carmody, Anne Fitzgerald, Susan Curtiss, Dugan Laird, and Geoffrey Bellman for reading our earlier draft of this work, and for providing us with invaluable feedback.

Preface

During the past several years we have each had occasion to prepare, design, and lead many workshops. We have also had the opportunity to participate in several workshops; some were positive experiences and others were negative experiences. The most successful workshops we attended seemed to have certain elements in common. They were well-organized, exciting, fulfilling, and informative. We left feeling satisfied, having grown both personally and professionally. The least successful workshops we attended seemed to be disorganized, dull, and irrelevant. We left feeling that we had wasted our time and money. Most of the workshops in which we participated, however, tended to fall in between those two extremes, being unmemorable due to their mediocrity. It is our belief, and our intention in this book, to illustrate that workshops can be highly positive and memorable experiences as long as they are carefully prepared and designed, and led with style and grace.

A delicious and elegant meal consists of three parts: careful preparation, meticulous cooking, and proper serving. It is then ready to be eaten and digested. Highly successful workshops also consist of three analagous parts: careful preparation, meticulous design, and proper leading. The quality of the digestive experience is proportional to the quality of those three parts. This book is actually a cookbook. Although practice and experience will enhance your skill greatly, if you follow the guidelines and the steps we describe you will be well on your way to becoming a highly skilled workshop designer and leader.

The purpose of this book is to provide a practical model for planning and running a workshop. We define *workshop* as a scheduled seminar in some specialized field, that has primarily a participatory approach to learning. What we refer to as a workshop, others may refer to as a seminar, course, class, discussion group, or laboratory experience.

The book is divided into three major sections: in the first we discuss the preparation involved in creating a workshop—the elements you need to consider before actually designing; in the second we describe and list the steps involved in the actual design process; in the third we discuss and list the important aspects involved in leading workshops. Our model is applicable to short and long workshops—to those lasting as little as one hour to those lasting several hundred hours. We believe this model has universal application when designing a program of learning in a specialized field, which has primarily a participatory approach to learning. This book should be useful to various groups of people, including—but in no way limited to—counselors, teachers, human relations consultants, human resource management trainers, management specialists, hospital personnel, and clergy. We are convinced that using this model will help you create well-organized, exciting, and fulfilling workshops.

PREPARING, DESIGNING, LEADING & WORKSHOPS

Overview

HUMANISTIC LEARNING: DEFINITION AND BELIEFS

The title of this book is *Preparing, Designing, and Leading Workshops: A Humanistic Approach.* We believe that people learn best when a humanistic approach is used. The term *humanistic* has been used frequently in the past several years by people in industry, education, and mental health. Much has been written about "humanistic education." It is often unclear, however, what the writer or speaker means when he or she employs this term. Therefore we would like to discuss what is meant by "humanistic approach," and to share with the reader how these humanistic beliefs influence the design of workshops. In this book we use the terms *trainer* or *teacher* to refer to the person who has the responsibility of designing and leading the workshop or course. The terms *participants, students,* or *trainee* are used in reference to those people who come to the workshop to gain new information.

A HUMANISTIC APPROACH

Students learn best when their **'whole person'** is involved in the learning process—the **intellectual, emotional, physical,** and **spiritual** parts of themselves.

The intellectual self refers to that part of oneself that thinks, solves problems, and is able to reason. The intellectual self is responsible for cognitive functioning. Most people enjoy having their minds stimulated, and an effective workshop both appeals to and stimulates the intellectual self.

The emotional self refers to the feeling part of oneself. Feelings are manifested in bodily sensations. There are four primary categories of feelings. They are anger, sadness, fear, and joy. The kinds of feelings people experience, and the depth of those feelings, vary constantly. An individual can be angry one minute, sad the next, and joyful shortly thereafter. Often people deny or block their feelings, although their feelings strongly influence their behavior. Since we are emotional beings, an effective workshop needs to pay attention to and be responsive to the feelings of the participants. Learning experiences

1

that help participants become aware of and responsive to their feelings encourage participants to be more in touch with their emotional selves.

The physical self refers to one's body, or any part of one's body. The physical self and the emotional self are usually connected. People's tensions, anxieties, fears, and conflicts often get manifested in their bodies and result in pain, chronic tension, disease, fatigue, etc. Conversely, taking care of one's body by eating nutritiously, sleeping well, and exercising regularly, contributes to feelings of well-being and emotional health. Participating in a workshop lacking physical activity can lead to a state of low energy levels, fatigue, or bodily tension. It is important, particularly in a workshop over two hours in length, to build in some physical activity. Standing up, moving around, finding a partner for a particular exercise, and breaking up into small groups, are movements that will aid the physical self.

The spiritual self refers to one's essence, or higher self. It is the part of the self that is able to see beyond one's own existence, that is able to find meaning in life and in the world around oneself. There are many ways to nourish the spiritual self such as listening to music, reading, writing, meditating, and taking walks. However, in a workshop, it is not always possible to pay a lot of attention to people's spiritual selves. Meditations, writing exercises, or time alone to absorb material, are some ways in which group leaders can incorporate some spirituality into their workshop. Traditional teaching methods generally appeal to the intellectual side of students, the assumption being that all four parts are unrelated, and that only the intellectual process is important in learning. We share the belief of many educators and psychotherapists including Rogers, Maslow, Moustakas, and Perls that all these parts of a person are connected and that learning can and does occur on any or all of these levels of functioning. Most people operate primarily out of one of these modes, and often that mode gets developed at the expense of the others. Sometimes, but not always, it is possible to reach all four parts of a person in a given workshop. The more parts you reach, the better. Often an idea that is presented cognitively cannot be fully grasped until the student has experienced it emotionally, perhaps through an experiential exercise.

Helping people feel positively towards themselves is an important and essential part of the learning process. Our experience is that most of us learn to compete with other students, and a teacher's emphasis is more often on what we do not do well, rather than on what we do well, and on what we know, rather than on who we are. We probably feel badly about ourselves more often than we feel good about ourselves. Therefore, we believe that trainers need to build up, not break down students' self-concepts. The better we feel about ourselves, the more quickly we will learn.

We believe that **people bring to learning situations many of their own resources,** which may or may not be developed, but which nevertheless exist. Traditional teachers often assume students come to courses empty headed about the particular subject they will learn. We cannot remember participating in or teaching a workshop in which the students knew nothing about the content. Students often believe they know nothing, but in the course of the workshop they discover they already have some knowledge of the subject matter. We believe students are teachers as well as learners; it is important to make time for them to share with each other and with the teacher what they already know. In that way everyone's knowledge is increased and students view themselves as intelligent, creative people.

The teacher is also a learner. Even though he or she is generally looked upon as the expert in a particular subject, the teacher certainly does not have all the answers. He or she can often learn from the students. If the teacher operates from this perspective, the students are more free to express their own ideas. The more students are able to express themselves, the less the gap between teacher and students. This atmosphere of shared learning helps students feel more comfortable, and that comfort helps them to learn more easily.

Another important belief we have about the humanistic learning process is that **students have unlimited potential to grow and change and absorb new information.** Jacobson and Rosenthal (1968)* have shown that when teachers were told that particular students (as indicated by intelligence tests) were expected to show a marked increase in learning over a given year, they in fact did so. Actually the particular students were randomly selected so it was not clear that they or any other students would show an increase in intellectual growth. The study clearly demonstrated that a teacher's expectations about a student's potential for intellectual growth is a strong indication of how much the student will learn. As teachers, we are not gods. We

---

*Jacobson and Rosenthal, *Pygmalion in the Classroom,* 1968.

have no knowledge of how much a student can or will achieve. It seems reasonable to assume that each of us, therefore, has an unlimited potential to take in new information and to grow as human beings in that process.

Finally, **participants have a primary responsibility for their own learning.** They play an active role in the learning process. Although ultimately what is taught and how it is taught is up to the teacher, students have an obligation to make their learning needs known, and have a right to see them met. Teachers should assess student's needs before actually beginning their design, and, as much as possible, incorporate these needs into the learning process. In addition to an initial assessment, there should be ongoing feedback between teacher and students that is not only elicited but is also taken into account. The teacher is the person who will have the primary responsibility for determining the content, designing the course, and teaching it. However, the teacher is making a mistake if he or she does not take students' needs and opinions seriously.

These concepts are how we define the term a **humanistic approach.** We take the learning process very seriously; it is, in its greatest form, an all encompassing growth experience for both the teacher and the learner.

UNDERLYING VALUES

With an understanding of the humanistic approach, we will now share our values and beliefs about the design process. **A good design is essential in running a successful workshop.** Creating a good design involves careful preparation on the part of the trainer. As we think of the most successful training experiences in which we have participated, it is clear they were well organized and carefully thought out ahead of time. The trainer let the participants know in the beginning of the workshop what they could expect to learn. As the workshop progressed each experience seemed to flow from the previous one, and each seemed to lead into the next. In short, the workshop had a design, a plan, and a direction in which it was heading.

As we reflect back on our participation in previous workshops in which we felt our time was wasted, it seems clear they were poorly organized and did not appear to be carefully thought out in advance. There were little, if any, connections between the different parts of the workshop. We entered and left confused about what we had learned, or at least confused about how to put it together. Again, it is our belief that a good design is key to a successful workshop, and that the trainer must be willing to put in the necessary preparation.

The process of design is easily taught. In our attempt to demystify this process, we have created a model that is simple and easy to follow. Often workshop trainers convey an inappropriate sense of specialness—that designing and leading workshops requires certain skills most people do not have. We believe designing and leading are separate skills that require different kinds of preparation, and that most people have the ability to do both. We are convinced that most people can learn how to be effective designers and leaders. Certainly the more experience you have in designing and leading, the less preparation you will need in order to design and lead a workshop. Although the step-by-step approach to designing that we outline may at times seem tedious and time-consuming, be assured that the time you spend in preparation will diminish as your skills in designing increase.

There is always uncertainty inherent in the process of designing and leading a workshop. You will not know for sure, until the workshop is completed, whether or not your design and leadership were effective. The process itself involves trial and error. Deleting goals due to lack of time, substituting one method for another, and changing certain structural arrangements are all part of designing and leading. It is perfectly okay for you to wonder how well your design will work in practice. If possible, let yourself wonder, rather than being anxious about it.

Several recent manuals that describe structured experiences are appropriate to use in most learning situations.[1] These manuals can be extremely useful resources in terms of methods, and are helpful to have when you design. It is our belief, however, that lists of structured experiences are only helpful if you are familiar with the steps involved in the design process. In fact, **if you know how to design, it is possible to plan a workshop relying solely on your own resources and creativity,** without having to depend on training manuals for your ideas. Feel free to use manuals, they can be quite helpful, but they are no substitute for your own fresh ideas.

---

[1]For example, Pfeiffer and Jones, *Structured Experiences for Human Relations Training.* University Associates Press, 1970.

It is important to **create a fresh design each time you lead a workshop.** Just as it is erroneous to assume another trainer's effective design will guarantee an effective workshop for you, it is also a mistake to assume a design you created for a previously successful workshop will be effective if used again. When teaching a subject you have taught before, it is tempting to pull an "old design" out of your files. However every learning experience is different. Therefore, use your previous designs as resources to create a fresh design since every group is a unique experience and demands its own design. Even if you wind up designing a workshop that is almost identical to one you have previously given, you have put fresh thoughts and ideas into it, which surely will be reflected in your teaching.

Finally, designing and leading workshops is a process that to some extent is mechanical, but to a much greater extent is creative, and demands a good deal of time and effort on the part of the trainer. Although we believe it is absolutely essential to follow the steps we outline in the process of designing a workshop, we believe this process is more than just the five steps. And, although we believe it is essential to exhibit the qualities and behaviors we describe in the leadership section, the process of leading involves more than these qualities and behaviors. Ideally this process is holistic, as is the learning process, involving the physical, emotional, intellectual, and spiritual energies of the designer/leader.

PREPARING FOR THE WORKSHOP
identifying the key elements

1

As you think about designing a workshop you might discover your-self reflecting on learning experiences you had that were exciting, informative, and made a lasting impression. You probably recall those learning experiences that you felt were a waste of time, boring, or had potential but were poorly planned and disorganized. If you focus your attention on those former workshop experiences, comparing and contrasting them, looking at their strengths and weaknesses, certain positive characteristics will emerge. These characteristics are the key elements that contribute to an exciting and meaningful workshop design.

Making a delicious meal involves some preparation before the cooking process begins. Ingredients may need to be chopped, seasoned, cut, thawed, or given some preparatory treatment before they can be cooked. Designing and leading workshops, as in cooking and serving a delicious meal, involves careful preparation, which ultimately enhances the flavor.

We have sifted through our years of experience in leading and par-ticipating in workshops to locate and identify **those ingredients that contribute to the excellence of a workshop experience.** We call these ingredients **the elements.** This chapter identifies the essential elements in designing and explains both what they are and how they are useful in planning a successful workshop. These elements need to be considered before you begin to design, as well as during the actual design process.

GATHERING INFORMATION ABOUT PARTICIPANTS

Gathering information about participants is the first element to consider when beginning to create your design. As trainer, you can often get caught up in your own excitement over the material you pre-sent. This excitement is an important ingredient in creating a suc-cessful workshop. What you need to remember, however, is that par-ticipants may have needs which differ from yours. Therefore gathering information about your participants, particularly their needs and wants, will help you to plan a workshop that is congruent with their needs as well as with your own. What follows is a discussion of the various questions to consider when gathering information about par-ticipants.

- What is the size of the group?
- How familiar are participants with the subject matter?
- What is the gender of the participants?
- What are the belief systems of participants?
- What are the learning needs and wants of participants?
- Is the workshop voluntary or mandatory?
- How well do the participants know one another?

The first question you need to ask is:

What is the size of the group with which you will be working?

Group size greatly influences how you will organize your workshop and what kind of experiences you will plan. There is a significant difference between conducting a workshop with ten people compared with a workshop of twenty or fifty. People are generally more reluctant to talk personally in a larger group; smaller groups are more conducive to personal sharing. The trainer also prepares himself or herself differently depending on the amount of people in the workshop. For example, one of the authors remembers an incident in which she thought she was giving a workshop for twenty people. She prepared a design that involved much physical movement and personal sharing. When she entered the room, she was surprised to find ninety people. She was not prepared psychologically, nor was her design geared for this large a group. The size of the group she expected influenced the type of tasks selected, the structure chosen for exchanging information, and the process selected to evaluate and integrate the learning. More careful research would have prevented this problem.

The second area to consider is:

How familiar are the participants with the subject matter?

Is the subject matter familiar to them or is it brand new? Gaining this information beforehand helps you to plan accordingly. If you assume the audience knows very little about the subject you are presenting and this assumption turns out to be false, you may discover you are boring your audience. On the other hand, if you assume they know a great deal, or should know a great deal and they do not, they may not be able to best utilize the teachings in the workshop. For example,

Preparing for the Workshop

suppose you are offering a Leadership Skills Workshop to supervisors in a mental health setting. Since they are supervisors you assume they have received some basic training in leadership. As you conduct the workshop, you discover they have had no formal training and, in fact, are feeling uncomfortable about doing a job for which they feel inappropriately trained. Collecting data prior to the workshop enables you to design a learning experience that fits the actual needs of the participants, not their imagined needs. Data collecting on leadership skills might include these considerations: How many people do you supervise? Has there ever been an in-service training program? If so, what topics were covered? If not, do you think it would be valuable? If so, how? As supervisors, what areas cause you the most difficulties?

In another situation you may be giving an Assertiveness Skills Workshop and assume that the participants are taking the workshop because they know nothing about being assertive. This is certainly a false assumption since most of us have either seen someone being assertive or have been assertive ourselves and are merely unaware of the assertive skills we possess. This informal process of learning is often not valued by participants. Therefore, the trainer's task is not only to present new information but also to demonstrate to participants how much knowledge they already possess.

The next question to consider is:

What is the gender of the participants?

Is your audience all women, all men, or mixed? If a workshop is limited to members of the same sex, you need to ask yourself whether issues or concerns particular to that sex will generally be more predominant. For example, if you are offering a Management Training Workshop to a group of women you would find that although women share some of the same concerns as male managers, they also have separate concerns from their male counterparts. Examples of female-oriented concerns are: how to manage men; problems in working in a predominantly male environment; coping with myths about women in business, etc.

If you are offering a Human Sexuality Workshop to a male and female group you would probably address concerns that deal with relationship issues: sexually understanding the opposite sex, communicating sexual wants, etc. Your design is not always influenced by the sex of the participants, although you may discover, as with the above examples, that it might be. The age of participants, marital status, and ethnicity are also factors that may influence your design.

The next question to consider is:

What are some of the belief systems of the participants?

Are there any strong attitudes among participants that could either enhance or detract from the workshop experience? Information about participants' attitudes and beliefs may be difficult to acquire. If you are hired by an organization, institution, or business, and do a little investigating, you can get a sense of the underlying values and beliefs of the system. It is true that assumptions based on limited data can be harmful, yet if you are aware of the danger of making assumptions you can let yourself make them and be willing to give them up if proven wrong.

How people respond to new experiences, like training, is influenced by their social, ethnic, religious, and political orientations. Organizations frequently have a social and political value system that is common knowledge. Knowing some of the values you may encounter will assist you in planning a design congruent with your material and responsive to the needs of the organization you are servicing.

If during a training program a participant rejects or resists a concept, you might ask yourself if this concept is dissonant with the belief system of the participant. If so, you may find a way to communicate your message without providing too much dissonance, remembering that new experiences, though exciting, are also risky, challenging, and potentially threatening. For example, if you were to conduct an Assertiveness Training Workshop for Right To Life proponents and you present the belief that every woman has the right to determine what she wants to do with her body, you may find yourself in the midst of a heated philosophical argument. With further thought you might present your idea in a way that would not be in direct conflict with the belief system of the organization. You might state, "We believe that women have the right to assert themselves and to strive for what they want." This latter statement is more general and gets the point across without being in conflict with the organization's value system. We know change produces anxiety; therefore, ideas that may be different from one's belief system will produce some level of discomfort, as illustrated by the above example. If you attempt to understand your audience's beliefs and values, and treat these beliefs and values with respect, you will facilitate the process of learning.

The next question to consider when gathering information about prospective participants is:

What are the learning needs or wants of the participants?

One way in which to imagine what some participants want from the workshop experience is to place yourself in the role of the participant. For example, you may offer a workshop to teachers entitled, "Managing Difficult Behavior." You could ask yourself: What issues would I like to see covered in this workshop? What subjects and feelings would I like to express and hear others discuss? By imagining yourself as a participant you will expand your awareness as to what to include in the design.

Another way to identify possible needs of participants is to take an informal survey of people you know. Ask them what topics they would like to see covered if they were to participate in a Managing Difficult Behavior Workshop. There are no guarantees that the actual participants will have the same needs as those you questioned, but it is still a good beginning for gathering information. A final suggestion is to ask people as they register for the workshop, what made them choose this workshop? What would they like to see happen, and what skills would they hope to have acquired when the experience is over? We call this process of gathering information **needs assessment.**

Another question to consider is:

Is this workshop voluntary or mandatory?

It makes a significant difference. People often resent others telling them they have to attend a workshop. Potential resentment can affect the tone of the workshop. If you are faced with this kind of situation, it is better to find it out ahead of time. If that is not possible, inquire during the first session. Required workshops initially have a different atmosphere. The participants can be more ambivalent, resistant, and difficult. Addressing this problem at the outset is one way of respecting the participants. Expressing concern for their situation and dealing directly with how to make the workshop a positive experience often reduces people's negative feelings. Participants' feelings are being respected; therefore, they are likely to be more open to begin the workshop with a positive outlook. Of course, you may be lucky enough to be giving a required workshop in which participants are eager to learn. If participants are attending the workshop out of choice, you will notice a different atmosphere, which is generally more receptive, in which expectations are higher, and attitudes are more positive.

The final question for consideration is:

How well do the participants know each other?

If people do not know each other some introductory exercises help group members to meet one another, and to feel more comfortable and relaxed. For example, at a recent Stress Reduction Workshop for managers, the leader recognized that it would be difficult and awkward for the participants, who came from various organizations. and settings, to share their feelings and thoughts after different exercises. Everyone present wanted to learn about stress reduction. Before they could allow themselves to get involved with the material, however, they needed to establish some contact with at least a few individuals in order to feel more at ease. Therefore, the leader designed experiences to help people get to know each other, establishing a safe climate for self-disclosure, and providing time to get acclimated to the new setting. Even if people know one another, it is still useful to provide some exercises that help group members to acknowledge relationships that already exist.

The above are the essential factors with which a designer should concern himself or herself regarding gathering information about participants.

FUN

Fun is the second element to consider when planning your design. There is a belief in our culture, commonly referred to as the Protestant Work Ethic—that in order to learn one has to work very hard and there is little fun involved in the process. "Grin and Bear It" was, for years, the general motto for students who complained that teachers made the learning process routine, dull, and boring. Our belief is that the very act of **learning itself can be exciting, creative, and fun.** We have observed that people learn best and remember most when they are having fun. Transactional analysts identify the part of self most receptive to fun as the child part. That "child" is intuitive, spontaneous, eager for excitement, and curious. Your design can excite the "child" that lives in all of us.

If participants tune out or are bored, it is usually the child part of the self that is dissatisfied and looks for another way to be entertained. This can take the form of fantasizing, making lists, or talking to others. Teachers and other leaders often label such a dissatisfied student as obnoxious, disinterested, or a troublemaker. In order to involve the participants, whether through experiences or lecturettes, it is crucial to remember it is the "child" part that can sabotage or encourage learning. The more you allow yourself to have fun as trainer, the more you give your participants permission to do the same.

TIME

Time is the third element you need to consider when planning your design. Beginning designers are often plagued with the fear that they will not have enough time or they will have too much time. Once again, there are certain questions to consider when designing. The first question is:

How much time are you allotted?

You may have much to say and several experiences you would like to provide and only have three hours. On the other hand, you may be giving a week long workshop and have ample time to cover a subject or develop a theme. A second question to ask is:

Are you building in time for reflection and integrating the workshop experience?

Even in a three-hour workshop, participants need time to reflect. This time is just as fruitful as is listening to a lecture or participating in an exercise. Longer workshops usually provide more opportunity to reflect and integrate. A third question to ask is:

Are you taking into account the slippage factor?

You may plan an exercise to take thirty minutes when in reality it takes fifty. It is, therefore, important to allow for slippage so you do not create a rushed atmosphere. It is better to do less than to rush through the material so you can feel that you 'got it all in'. The last consideration is:

Are you building in time for breaks?

We can get overloaded with ideas and feelings; coffee breaks and informal time need to be built into your design.

APPROPRIATE SEQUENCING

The fourth major area to consider when designing is whether there is an **appropriate sequence** to the design. **A design should have a natural flow.** Letting yourself be sensitive to the overall picture you have created will help you determine if there is a flow, or if your design is merely a series of experiences that do not relate well to each other or create a sense of wholeness. Some leaders who are new at using experiential techniques often introduce a series of exercises that remains just that, a series of exercises. In your design, attempt to create a sequence of events so that both you and the participants can see how the previous exercise relates to the next, and how it fits into the larger picture.

Sequencing Format

Designing a workshop is in one sense like creating a play or preparing a speech. There is a beginning, a middle, and an end, or as in a speech, there is an **introduction,** a **body,** and a **conclusion.** The purposes of the introduction, body, and conclusion suggest a methodology for achieving a natural sequencing in designing workshops. The **introduction** or beginning of a workshop has several functions:

1. to gain the attention of participants,
2. to introduce participants and leader(s) to one another,
3. to discuss the format of the workshop, and
4. to build excitement and interest in the material that follows.

The following are examples of exercises that respond to the first two purposes of the introduction. We call these **icebreaker exercises.**

This exercise is probably appropriate for groups of up to thirty people. Ask the participants to sit in a circle. The first person says his or her first name. The next person says the name of the person who spoke, pauses a few seconds, then says his or her first name. The third person says the name of the person who first spoke, then the name of the second person who spoke, pauses, and states his or her name. This procedure continues until everyone in the circle has the opportunity to say the names of the participants before them as well as their own names. If someone forgets the name of a person who spoke earlier, that person repeats his or her name once again.

A second game for learning names utilizes a ball or other throwable object. It is probably appropriate for groups of not more than twenty people. Ask participants to form a circle. Someone begins by throwing the ball to another person in the circle. As the first person throws the ball, he or she calls out his or her name. The person then catches the ball and throws it to another person while saying his or her name. The ball continues to be thrown around the circle while the throwers call out their names. After everyone has thrown the ball a couple of times, the directions change. This time as participants throw the ball they say the name of the person to whom they are throwing it. Continue the game until everyone's name is familiar, or until the excitement wanes.

These two exercises are examples of how participants can learn each other's names. These exercises are fun and they tend to increase participants' excitement. In addition, they help the participants and the leaders establish contact with one another. We encourage you to design other icebreaker exercises for learning names.

If you decide you would like participants to get more acquainted with each other rather than just learning names, the following suggestions might be useful. These introductions can take up to an hour and are particularly appropriate for lengthy workshops in which participants will spend a great deal of time together.

Suggestions for Getting Acquainted

- Ask participants to turn to the person next to them and spend ten minutes getting to know one another.
- Ask participants to choose a partner and discuss what has brought each of them to the workshop.
- Ask participants to talk about their expectations for the workshop and to identify some learning goals they have for themselves.

When using any of these three suggestions you can ask group members to introduce their partners to the group and share some of the information they obtained.

Once again, these exercises are only suggestions to help stimulate your own creative thought processes. We encourage you to use your own creativity, and design getting acquainted exercises that will suit the participants in the workshop you are offering. It is important, however, to first decide how much time you would like to spend on this part of the design.

After participants have been introduced to each other, it is important to spend a few minutes discussing the format of the workshop. Whether the workshop is two hours, or several days in length, participants will want to have some idea about what they can hope to gain from attending the workshop. One method of sharing this information is to talk about the goals for the workshop. (See Establishing Goals under "Designing Workshops".) Somehow you need to **let participants know what to expect.** It is also important to discuss business procedures—starting and ending times, lunch, breaks, and any other relevant details. Discussing these issues at the beginning of a group usually helps participants feel oriented, and helps to build excitement and interest in the material that follows.

The overall purpose of the **body** of the workshop is to cover the material that relates to the goals of the workshop. The **body** consists of two primary functions:

1. teaching concepts
2. practicing skills

The material can be presented in the form of lecturettes, structured and nonstructured experiences, discussions, and processing. (See Selecting Methods and Structures under "Designing Workshops".) As in a play, the body is where the plot is developed and the characters are defined. The body is the heart of the workshop and thus answers the following questions: (1) What is the purpose of the workshop? and (2) What ideas and skills am I attempting to teach?

The major functions of the **conclusion** of a workshop are as follows:

1. to focus the thoughts of the participants on the central themes and purposes of the workshop
2. to highlight the essential points
3. to allow for feedback
4. to convey a sense of completeness and finality

People learn best when central concepts are repeated several times in new and different ways. Designing a conclusion that will in some way **highlight the central goals** should help to reinforce the learning experience. An exercise designed to highlight the important learnings for participants helps them to integrate these learnings. **Helping participants identify their learnings** also aids them in gaining a sense of closure.

The end of the workshop is also a time to **ask for feedback** about the workshop and to allow participants to **give feedback** to each other as well as to the leader(s). Sharing reactions is a way to highlight specific learnings. In addition, giving and receiving feedback contributes to a sense of closure. (See Evaluation under "Preparing Workshops".)

The concluding portion of the workshop needs to clearly **communicate that the workshop has ended.** Too often trainers end because time has run out, in which case there is no time to tie up loose ends and focus on those functions, previously mentioned, that contribute to a good ending. You may, during the conclusion of the workshop, think of some ideas you want to add. Be careful though, not to overload the participants with new data when they are trying to experience a sense of completeness.

INTRODUCTION
- gain participant's attention
- introduce leader(s) and participants
- discuss format
- build excitement and interest

BODY
- teach concepts
- practice skills

CONCLUSION
- focus on central themes
- highlight essential points
- allow for feedback
- convey completeness

The following are examples of exercises that can help you in concluding a workshop, and that address the different purposes of the conclusion.

- Ask participants to take a moment to select a few adjectives that describe their experience of being in this workshop.

- Ask participants to identify what parts of the workshop were the most useful and the least useful for them.
- Ask participants to identify what the biggest surprise was for them while attending the workshop.
- Ask participants to select one concept they learned that they can apply tomorrow when they return to work.

Once again, the above exercises are only suggestions for ways to conclude a workshop. Try making up some of your own. If you follow the theory that an effective workshop has a beginning, a middle, and an end, and if you respond to the functions of each of these parts, you will surely create a natural sequence to your design.

Sequencing Principles

There are four basic sequencing principles to which you need to pay attention when designing. The first principle is that **some skills need to be mastered first before others.** For example, one needs to develop good listening skills before learning to be confrontative, because learning how to accurately hear what is being said leads to clearer communication and more effective confrontations. If confrontation is necessary, you first need to be sure you have fully heard what has been said to you. Therefore, if you are teaching a course on "Counseling Skills," it is important that participants be able to listen well to what is being communicated before developing confrontative skills.

A second guideline for creating an appropriate sequence is to **teach easier concepts first before teaching more difficult ones.** Generally, we learn more easily when one idea is an outgrowth of another. Beginning with simpler concepts provides a foundation for teaching more difficult ideas and skills. For example, when learning mathematics, we need to first master the skills of multiplication and division before learning fractions and decimals. In learning how to write words, we first need to learn the alphabet. The same principle is true in workshops. If we are teaching a seminar on communication skills, it makes sense to first teach active listening techniques before teaching people how to give and receive feedback. If, as designers, we think in terms of what skill needs to come first, as well as what skills are easier to master than others, then we are applying appropriate sequencing principles to designing.

A third principle of sequencing is to **ask participants to practice less**

risky skills before asking them to practice more risky ones. For example, it is easier when teaching supervisory skills, to ask participants to role-play talking to an employee about his tardiness, then to tell him he is being fired. Most of the same skills are involved in either situation. Dealing with tardiness, however, is less emotionally stressful and risky, than is terminating someone's employment.

A fourth guideline for appropriate sequencing is to **provide a demonstration before asking participants to practice a skill.** For example, if you are leading a workshop on Interviewing Techniques for managers, it is important to teach interviewing concepts and to give a demonstration before asking participants to practice their interviewing skills. Demonstrations are particularly helpful when you are working with a large group, since you will probably not be able to provide much individual attention. It is also helpful to conduct a demonstration when a skill is particularly complicated and difficult. Demonstrating a technique or a skill can help communicate it in a much clearer way, which will often make the participants' practice session easier and more satisfying. It is important to remember that many people learn best when they can see a skill actually being demonstrated.

Demonstrations are also useful when working with participants who are easily threatened by practicing unfamiliar skills. Comprehending instructions, and putting theory into practice without first seeing how it is done is often quite confusing for some people. For other people practicing a new skill can be quite threatening. Therefore, a demonstration provides an opportunity for greater understanding, before participants try out the new idea or skill on their own.

There is, however, an exception to the principle of demonstrating skills before practicing. You may at some time wish to ask participants to practice a skill, for example, conducting an interview, before actually providing any theory. In this case your purpose would be to help them identify what interviewing skills they already possess and what skills they are lacking. Theory can then be generated from the participants' discussion of how they actually conducted the interview. As you listen to participants discuss the strategies they used, as well as what was effective and ineffective, you can interject appropriate theory.

Some people learn best by hearing a concept explained, others by seeing it demonstrated, and still others by actually practicing it. Therefore, when developing an appropriate sequence in your design, make sure that **fundamental concepts come first, easier concepts come before more difficult ones, low risk-taking comes before high risk-taking, and demonstrations come before practice.**

- Some skills need to be mastered before others
- Teach easier concepts before more difficult ones
- Ask participants to practice less risky skills first
- Provide a demonstration before asking participants to practice

SIMPLICITY

Beginning designers often make their designs too complex. Therefore, **simplicity** is the fifth element to consider. **The design needs to be easily understood by you and your participants.** If there are too many directions, people generally get confused and frustrated. If there are too many steps to follow in order to get the point, the point often gets lost. The easier and simpler the design is, the greater the chance of success. If you have to read it over several times yourself, it is probably not simple enough. If you find yourself having to give directions in two or three different ways, the directions are probably not clear.

VARIETY

Variety is the sixth element of designing. Since **people learn, and are motivated by different means,** it is important that your design have variety. In this section we identify five ways in which workshop designs can be varied:

1. by using a holistic approach (the involvement of people's emotional, intellectual, physical, and spiritual selves)
2. by varying the length of different segments
3. by using different mediums
4. by varying the intensity of different experiences
5. by varying the structure of the experiences

It is essential to add variety to your design in order to capture people's interests and to facilitate their learning.

The emotional self is captured by experiences that allow participants to become aware of their feelings. It is then important to provide opportunities for participants to express these feelings. For example, let us assume you are offering a workshop on "Leadership

Preparing for the Workshop

21

Skills'' and you want to engage the emotional self. You might ask participants to make a list of ten qualities of an effective leader and ten qualities of an ineffective leader. Then ask participants to check those qualities, both positive and negative, that they believe they possess. Ask participants to share with each other in groups of three the qualities they feel they possess. In addition, ask them to discuss what it felt like to disclose this information about themselves to others. The following is another example that involves the emotional self. Assume you are offering a workshop entitled ''Finding the Ideal Job.'' As part of the workshop you might ask participants to imagine themselves working at a job where they feel angry most of the day. Then you could ask them to imagine themselves working at a job where they feel bored most of the day. Finally, you could ask them to imagine themselves at a job in which they feel happy most of the time. This exercise will help participants identify what job situations produce which types of feelings.

When you are engaging the intellectual self you are presenting information, teaching concepts and theories, analyzing models, and solving problems. When you are presenting a lecturette that involves theory, facts, or ideas, you are engaging the intellectual self. When you give a team of managers a problem to solve you are asking participants to employ their analytical skills, and you are therefore involving their intellectual selves. When you ask participants to apply a new theory to their current work situation you are asking them again to utilize their intellectual selves.

Another part of the self that needs to be involved at times during the workshop is the physical self. **Any experiences that necessitate bodily movement engage the physical self.** When the physical self is actively expressed there is usually a spurt of energy and vitality in the group. Movement helps to revitalize people and to provide further enthusiasm for the work to follow. For example, after lunch when people are often feeling sluggish, you may ask participants to do some stretching exercises or to play a short game such as tag. An enjoyable exercise that usually works well in a group of fairly uninhibited people is the following one. Ask participants to stand in a circle. One person begins by making a gesture and a sound that represents how he or she is currently feeling. The rest of the group imitates the gesture and the sound. Everyone in the group who wishes to, then has an opportunity to express himself or herself in this physical way. Participants get the chance to experience how other people are feeling.

The fourth part of the self is the spiritual self, sometimes called the higher self. **Experiences that ask people to focus their attention inwardly—such as meditation, guided fantasy, or relaxation exercises—engage the spiritual self.** Such experiences allow participants to become in touch with parts of themselves of which they are less aware. Usually, these experiences are quiet in nature and require people to be personally reflective. Not all workshops, however, utilize exercises which engage the spiritual self. Sometimes people feel awkward when they are asked to focus their attention inwardly. The following is an example of an experience that touches the spiritual self. Ask each participant to sit quietly for five minutes and observe his or her thoughts and feelings, and to be aware of any physical sensations. Encourage participants only to notice their thoughts, feelings, or sensations, rather than to become involved in, or responsive to them. This technique helps to clear people's minds, which in turn will aid in the learning process.

The second way to vary your design is to **vary the length of the different segments.** Some experiences may take one or even two hours, others may take thirty minutes, and still others may take only fifteen minutes to complete. You should plan to provide experiences which last different lengths of time. A series of very long exercises can be tiresome. A series of very short exercises might be confusing if too much material is presented in too short a time.

A third way to add variety to your design is to **vary your medium of communication whenever possible.** The media most often appropriate for use are crayons and paper for drawing, pen and paper for writing, clay for sculpting, and video-tape equipment and films for viewing. For example, if you are offering a workshop in "Team Building" to a division of managers, you could ask them to communicate how they work together by drawing a symbolic representation of their working relationship. Drawing is often a useful way to express feelings and impressions, particularly for people who have some difficulty expressing their feelings verbally. If you are offering a workshop on "Marriage Counseling," you could ask participants to make a sculpture using clay to represent how they view an ideal marriage. Using films or slides to stimulate thought and to evoke feelings and discussion, are additional ways to vary your design using different mediums. The participants will probably respond positively to your creative efforts.

Preparing for the Workshop

A fourth way to vary your design is through **intensity—the emotional feeling connected to a particular experience.** Some experiences are naturally 'lighter' than others, that is, they do not absorb a great amount of people's emotional energy. Other experiences are more intense, or 'heavy' and tend to require a great deal of participant's emotional energy. Experiences which move from lightness to more intensity affect the tone and mood of the group. Having several intense learning experiences in a row can leave participants drained. Having too many light experiences in a row may cause participants to become bored or restless. Therefore, vary the intensity of your design.

Finally, it is important to **vary the structures you use to implement your methods.** For example, a lecturette, followed by a small group discussion, followed by a two-person experience provides movement and change. Listening to a lecture for an extended period of time can be extremely boring, as well as physically tiring. On the other hand, working in a pair, or in a group of three can become too emotionally draining if the experience is prolonged. No matter what your format is, you need to vary it in order to hold participants' interest and to allow people to absorb the material in a way that is most helpful to them.

Appealing to the four aspects of self, varying the length of different time segments, using different mediums, varying the intensity of different experiences, and changing the structures of the experiences, are all ways to achieve variety in your design. Being a creative designer pays off. As a designer you are in some ways like a director of a play. It is important to involve the audience as much as possible using all of the five ways we discussed.

SHARING EXPECTATIONS

Sharing expectations is the seventh element to consider when planning your design. **Expectations—what the participants hope to gain from the workshop—fall into two major categories: content and structure.** To identify content expectations, allocate time at the beginning of the workshop to state your goals for the workshop and find out the expectations of the participants. In this way you can match participants' learning needs with what you have planned.

You could ask participants to list two things they want to gain from the workshop. You can then list all their wants on a blackboard or a piece of newsprint, and identify and discuss which areas will be covered and which ones will not. This enables participants to gain clarity about what they want to learn, helps them to verbalize their expectations, and checks their expectations against what you have already planned. Identification of needs helps to eliminate false expectations as well as to gain an opportunity at the beginning of the workshop to make changes if participants' learning needs are significantly different from your own.

Structural expectations deal with how the workshop will be organized in terms of time. Let participants know the format of the workshop. For example: "We will work for three hours in the morning starting at nine and ending at noon, have a two hour lunch break, resume at two and end at five." Responding to content and structural expectations prepares participants for the work to follow.

CLIMATE

The atmosphere, which we call climate, is the eighth element of design. **The climate contributes to feelings of comfort/discomfort, safety/danger, and intimacy/distance.** Therefore, create an appropriate climate for your workshop. There are **six physical factors to consider** when setting an atmosphere for learning. They are: **size of the physical space, level of comfort, lighting, temperature, furniture,** and **availability.** When looking for a place to conduct your workshop be sure to select a space that is conducive to the work you plan to do. The size of the room you select is important. If you have a large group you need to have enough space so people can spread out. This is particularly necessary if participants will be working in triads or in small groups. If you have a small group you do not want a room in which people get lost. People learn best when they are comfortable, therefore knowing ahead of time what the furniture is like (if there is any) is helpful. First, you want to know if the furniture is movable. Second, you need to determine if you want people to sit on chairs or mats and pillows. Many people who offer experiential workshops find that mats and pillows, which you probably will need to supply, are more comfortable than chairs, and create a more informal atmosphere. The way you arrange the furniture communicates a message to the participants. Setting up chairs in rows conveys a much different message than arranging them in a circle. Therefore, it is wise to arrive at the workshop site early to make sure the room is set up as you would like it to be. Lighting is a concern which often is given little forethought. Natural lighting is the best for a daytime activity. Some

The Elements in Designing

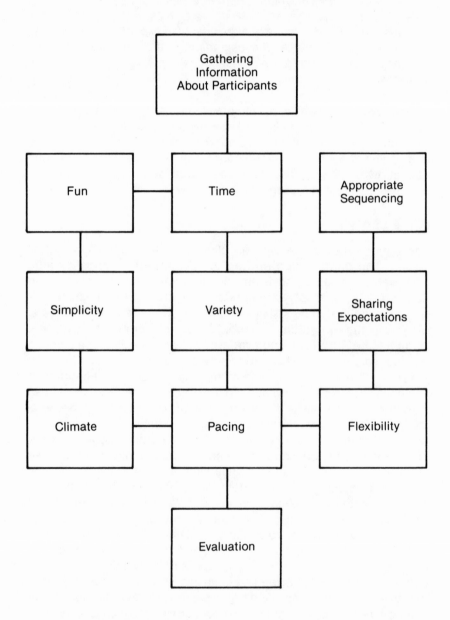

kinds of lighting are draining and tiring. If at all possible, spend some time in the room to determine how the lighting affects you. Another factor in creating a climate conducive to learning is temperature. Do you have control over the temperature? Is the room warm enough, too warm, and is there air conditioning if necessary? Finally, if you are giving a workshop several days in a row, or once a week for several weeks, you need to determine if the space you have chosen is available for the length of your workshop. People begin to settle into a working environment; changing locations is often difficult.

PACING

The ninth element of design is called pacing. We all have inner clocks that determine how we best take in information. No two person's inner clocks are the same. **Paying attention to your own timing, and the timing of the participants, allows you to alter the pacing when necessary.** Pacing, or rate of presentation, can be looked at in two ways. The first is how fast or slow you are talking. Do people look harried, bored, or relaxed and involved while you are speaking? If you sense participants are harried or bored it is best to check this assumption out with the group. You can directly ask, ''How are people doing with the pacing of the material?'' or ''Am I speaking too quickly, too slowly, or just fine?'' The second way pacing can be regarded is in terms of the exercises. Are you allowing enough time for a task to be completed or are you providing too much time and therefore losing the momentum of the workshop?

FLEXIBILITY

The tenth element is flexibility. **When you are planning the design and while you are actually conducting the workshop you need to be flexible.** If you have completed your design, and it does not seem right, even if you have put in a great deal of time, **trust your instincts and make some changes.** This is hard to do, but experience has taught us not to get too invested in our designs. If, while you are conducting the workshop, significant learnings and/or events are happening, it is important to know when to let go of parts of your planned design and when to make on-the-spot changes. It is helpful to remember that some experiences take more time or have more impact than you imagined. Measure the importance of what is happening in terms of its relevance to your goal. Being sidetracked can be interesting and creative and it can also cause difficulties; some participants may become frustrated because they cannot see the relevance of the discussion in terms of the workshop goals. In those instances, it is usually better to go back to the original design. However, if a subject is taking longer than you thought, or has gone in a direction you didn't anticipate but is supportive of the goal, then it is better to be flexible. Preparing yourself emotionally to make changes eliminates the feelings of panic if a change is deemed necessary.

EVALUATION

The final element of design is evaluation. **There are two kinds of evaluation: ongoing and concluding.**

Ongoing Evaluations

It is important to **evaluate the workshop while it is still in progress.** Too often trainers evaluate a workshop only at the end, which does not provide an opportunity to make any changes. Periodic evaluations provide ongoing feedback to the trainer and give the participants an opportunity to integrate what they have learned. Evaluation in an ongoing workshop is geared toward identifying whether participants are learning from the workshop and enjoying themselves. Asking for feedback while the workshop is still in progress provides you with an opportunity to take the pulse of the group—to determine if the workshop is proceeding as you would like it to be. Plan to conduct several, or at least a few, ongoing evaluations during the course of the workshop. If you discover a change would be beneficial, perhaps a change in pace or in the format, you can take the time to make the needed alterations. Evaluating how people are feeling and whether their needs are being met can be done simply. The following are a few methods for evaluating the workshop while it is still in progress. They are all methods we have used and found to be helpful. Feel free to use them and to develop some of your own.

Suggestions for Ongoing Evaluation Questions

- Ask participants for a one word description of how they are feeling at the moment

This gives you, as trainer, a sense of the feeling tone of the group, which will give you a good idea of how people are responding to the workshop. You will discover whether people are excited, bored, distracted, anxious, etc.

- Ask the participants to think of an adjective which describes how they feel the workshop is going so far

By taking this pulse of the group you can determine whether a more lengthy evaluation is necessary. If the adjectives are primarily negative, you would probably want to conduct a more extensive evaluation in order to determine exactly what is wrong and what you can do about it.

- Ask participants to rate the workshop so far on a scale of one to ten, one representing very negative feelings and ten representing very positive feelings

This technique will help you assess how well-received and meaningful the workshop has been up to that point.

- Ask participants to identify what has been the most meaningful or most useful part of the workshop

This question might help you to decide what to include more of in your design.

If at any time you are wondering how people are reacting to a particular experience, ask them. It is appropriate to ask the following questions, or others that you may think of along the same lines.

- Are we spending enough or too much time on this topic or segment?
- Are you having any particular difficulties with this concept or exercise? If so, what?
- Are you ready to move on?

The best way to find out what participants are thinking, and how they are feeling about the workshop is to ask.

Ongoing evaluations prevent both you and participants from being unpleasantly surprised or disappointed at the end of the workshop. As previously mentioned, by taking the pulse of the group you can assess whether or not to make any changes. If you do make needed changes along the way, it is unlikely that the final evaluation will be anything but highly positive.

Concluding Evaluations

Another important kind of evaluation is a final or concluding evaluation. **It is essential to evaluate a workshop at its end.** Concluding evaluations differ from ongoing evaluations in that they are concerned with whether or not the workshop did in fact meet participants' expectations and satisfy the stated goals. Concluding evaluations help trainers get a picture of the workshop as a whole, as well as a sense of the various parts. A concluding evaluation also allows participants to provide feedback to you, as trainer, and to other group members as well. Everybody has an opportunity to directly express their feelings, thoughts, and reactions to you and to each other. In addition, concluding evaluations lend a sense of closure to the workshop. They can be written or oral. We prefer to include both. Although an evaluation needs to be geared to the specific workshop you are offering, the following suggestions are questions that can be easily adapted to most workshops and can be asked either in written or oral form. Feel free to use them, though be sure to include ones specifically tailored to your workshop.

Suggestions for Concluding Evaluation Questions

- What was the most useful part of this workshop? Why? What was the least useful part? Why?
- What made it easy for you to be here today? What made it difficult?
- What have you learned that you can use Monday morning when you return to work? What have you learned that will take more time to integrate?
- What appreciations, resentments, or regrets would you like to express before you leave here today? (When using this exercise be sure to limit discussion. Encourage people to express their thoughts and feelings, to listen to other people's, and to be receptive to feedback.)
- What are some tools/skills/ideas that you have now that you did not have when the workshop began?
- What final statements would you like to make to the workshop leader or to other participants?

As mentioned previously, an effective workshop has a sense of closure when it is time to end. Evaluating the workshop aids in the termination process. An evaluation is also an important tool for you as trainer. The feedback should help you plan future workshops so the quality of your next workshop will be even higher and it will come even closer to meeting the needs of the participants. It is important to treat this process very seriously, so be sure to allow enough time at the end of the workshop for a thorough concluding evaluation.

What has been provided in this section is a description of those elements a trainer needs to consider when designing and leading a workshop. To summarize, **the basic elements of design are: gathering information about the participants; having fun; knowing your time limits; appropriate sequencing; simplicity; variety; sharing expectations; climate setting; pacing; flexibility; evaluation.** If you pay attention to these elements before designing your workshop, and follow the five steps as described in the following chapter, you are likely to create an interesting and stimulating workshop.

DESIGNING THE WORKSHOP 2

In many ways designing a workshop is like cooking a meal. Once the ingredients are gathered and prepared they need to be cooked and arranged in the proper order. It is not enough to throw them all together in a dish, bake them in the oven, and hope the finished product will be a savory beef stroganoff or a chocolate layer cake. Ingredients need to be added, step by step, in an orderly process, so their chemical composition is correct. Only then will the finished product be attractive to view and tasty to the palate. It is therefore essential to follow the recipe closely—to combine the ingredients properly, and to cook them for the designated amount of time. Similarly, designing a workshop first requires preparing the ingredients (the elements). Next, it is essential to combine the ingredients with the proper methods, in the correct order. It is important that enough time be allowed for cooking (designing), since the task involved is to teach theory and concepts and transform ideas into skills and behavior.

Designing a workshop involves five important steps: **establishing goals; brainstorming methods; selecting methods and structures; evaluating the design; and revising the design.** In this section, we will attempt to explain the process of designing by going through these five steps.

ESTABLISHING GOALS

We define a goal as a behavioral result one strives to attain. The first and perhaps most important task in designing the workshop is to **establish your goals and to list them.** It is important to **be specific, be clear about what you are teaching, and to state your goals so that the results can be measured.** For example, let us assume your task is to design a ten-week Supervision Skills course for managers. The course will be offered to first line managers. Some examples of goals you might establish for the course are:

1. The participants will learn and demonstrate active listening skills.
2. The participants will learn and demonstrate interventions that help employees take responsibility for helping to solve their own problems.
3. The participants will learn to identify the difference between primary and secondary problems.
4. The participants will learn and demonstrate interventions that help employees become aware of their feelings about their jobs.

These are just some examples of goals you might have for the workshop. They are specific, they each speak to an end result you wish to achieve, and the results will be measurable.

Some examples of goals that would be too general are:

1. The participants will learn supervisory skills.
2. The participants will learn important concepts of supervision.

If the skills and concepts to which these general goals refer were listed separately, then each one would be specific enough. However, as stated above, the goals are too general and it would be difficult, if not impossible to measure results.

In order to measure results, **your goals must be stated in terms of behavioral outcomes.** You can determine whether or not the participants have met the goals established by checking for the desired behavior. For example, the way to evaluate if participants have met the goal "participants will learn to identify the difference between primary and secondary problems," is to present each participant with a work-related problem and ask him or her to differentiate between the employee's primary and secondary problems. If the participant is successful, then your objective has been realized. To measure the outcome of the "learn and demonstrate active listening skills" goal, observe the participant in a "supervisory" role and evaluate which interventions, as well as how many, meet the criteria you have set up for active listening.

Many people, in designing workshops, confuse goals and methods. Some examples of methods sometimes mistaken for goals are:

- Role playing
- Engaging in the listening repetition exercise
- Breaking into dyads
- Fishbowling

These are either methods, or structures, or means towards the attainment of a goal. They are not goals in themselves, as they do not describe an end result. For example, doing the listening repetition exercise might be a *method* to help the participants increase their listening skills, but it is not a *goal.*

Also in setting goals, **it is important to state goals in terms of what the participants will learn,** not what the trainers wish to accomplish.

Designing the Workshop

For example, as previously stated, one of the objectives you have established is, "The participants will learn interventions that help employees become aware of their feelings about their jobs." This goal is stated in terms of what the participants will be able to do when they have completed the workshop. An example of a goal that is *not* stated in terms of what the participants will be able to do is, "*To teach participants* how to make interventions that help employees become aware of their feelings about their jobs." Your intention as trainers is thus defined, but it is not clear what the participants will be able to do when they have completed your workshop.

Thus, establishing goals answers the questions:

- What do you wish to achieve?
- What do you want people to go away with?
- What do you want to see happen?

Setting goals gives the workshop direction and focus. Without them, participants will probably be confused about the overall concepts to be learned. Therefore, it is also important to share the goals you establish with the participants, preferably at the beginning of the workshop. Sharing goals can help establish the climate and prepare the participants for the experience they are about to have. (See "Sharing Expectations" under Elements.)

Once you have established your goals you need to **estimate the amount of time you will need in order to meet the goals.** In some instances, the workshop designer/leader is able to determine the length of time needed. This situation is ideal because you need not eliminate some goals due to lack of time. In these instances, it is probably best to determine the time needed after designing the entire workshop. If you need to determine the length of time, but are not in a position to complete the entire design, then you must make a rough approximation. Examine the selected goals and try to get a reasonable sense of how long it will take to meet them. In most situations, however, the amount of time for the workshop is already determined by the people who contract for it.

Assuming the time allotted for the workshop has already been determined, it is important, once you have set your goals, to decide if they can be met in that time limit. In a ten-week Supervision Skills Workshop for first-line managers, it is highly reasonable to assume you can achieve each of the four goals previously mentioned. In fact, you would probably add a few more. If, however, you were asked to teach a three-hour Supervision Skills Workshop to the same population, meeting all four goals would be a totally unreasonable expectation. Each goal is, in itself, enough material for a three-hour session. The more experience you have in designing and leading workshops, the easier it becomes to estimate how much you can achieve in the allotted time. It will save time if you can look at the goals you have enumerated and decide at that point if they can be met within the time limit.

It may happen, however, after planning the methods you will use to reach your goals, that it becomes clear there are too many goals. If that is the case, then you will need to eliminate some. Beginning designers, and sometimes even experts, have a tendency to try to include too much in their designs. In that case usually one of two things happens: the time may be up before the design is finished, the workshop is incomplete, and the participants leave without a sense of closure; or, if the leader realizes the error and rushes through the design in an endeavor to finish, the participants may leave feeling generally confused, having been unable to absorb much of the material.

If you discover you have set too many goals, then you need to prioritize them and set reasonable limits for yourself, which means eliminating some. Thus, the goals you finally do include will be the most important ones. It is necessary, however, to make a clear statement to the participants that you have selected the goals of primary concern to you, and that if more time were allotted you would also include others.

The last step in goal-setting is to **organize the goals in a logical flow.** Often, the acquisition of one skill presupposes the acquisition of another; or sometimes one experience, in order to be meaningful, needs to precede or follow another experience. In any case, it is important that the workshop be a whole entity with a beginning, a middle, and an end, rather than a series of unconnected exercises or experiences that do not fit together in a meaningful way. (See "Appropriate Sequencing" under Elements.) Thus, **goal-setting answers the question of WHAT your objectives will be.**

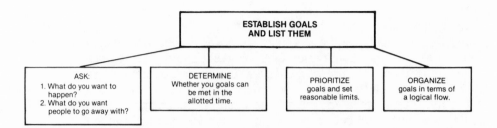

BRAINSTORMING METHODS

Once you have established your goals and organized them in a logical sequence, you are then ready to think of some possible methods for meeting these goals. We believe **the best way to come up with creative and exciting ideas is to "brainstorm."** The process of brainstorming is very simple. Starting with your first goal, list as many ideas for achieving the goal as you can think of, without judging each idea on its potential merit. Although it is tempting to evaluate the pros and cons of the methods as you list them, judging them prematurely tends to inhibit the number of ideas you might generate as well as inhibit your creativity. Brainstorming is a process that works well whether you are designing by yourself or with one or more people. So, the first rule of brainstorming is to **list as many ideas as possible, without judging each one.**

The second rule of brainstorming is to **be creative; assume the sky is the only limit.** You may later decide that a "way out" idea is exactly what you need to get your point across. At any rate, since you are not committed to using each of the ideas, it is to your advantage (and primarily to the participants' advantage) to brainstorm as many ideas as possible. Therefore, the methods you do select will be chosen from among many possibilities, and thus the probability of choosing the best possible method(s) is great.

The third rule in brainstorming is to **take off on your own or on other people's ideas.** Sometimes one suggestion triggers another. There is no patent on any one idea; in fact using other people's ideas and modifying them is encouraged. Suppose one of your goals in session #5 of the Supervision Skills Workshop is, "The participants will learn interventions that help employees become aware of their feelings about their jobs." First brainstorm methods you may use to meet this goal.

You might suggest asking participants to list the different kinds of body cues they experience when they feel sad, angry, afraid, and joyful. That idea may trigger a similar one: asking participants to list the different kinds of body cues they notice *other* people exhibiting when they feel sad, angry, afraid, and joyful. Thus, the second idea is similar to the first; however, it is also different, and would undoubtedly evoke a different response from the workshop participants.

Let us assume you and your co-leader continue brainstorming methods to use in teaching participants interventions that help employees become aware of their feelings about their jobs. Including the two ideas mentioned above, here is a list of some ideas we brainstormed:

1. Asking the participants to list the different kinds of body cues they experience when they feel sad, angry, afraid, and joyful.
2. Asking the participants to list the different kinds of body cues they notice other people exhibiting when others feel sad, angry, afraid, and joyful.
3. Conduct a fantasy in which the participants are asked to remember a time at work when they felt angry, sad, joyful, or afraid, and to notice where they felt those feelings in their bodies.
4. Ask the participants to focus on their breathing, to let go of their thoughts, and to be aware only of what they are feeling.
5. Introduce a sentence completion exercise focusing on feelings.
6. Ask participants to make two lists: one of thoughts and one of feelings.
7. Introduce a discussion about the difference between thoughts and feelings.
8. Do the SEE-IMAGINE-FEEL exercise (see page 43).
9. Give a lecturette on the difference between thoughts and feelings.
10. Ask participants to break into triads to role play a problem at work (one manager, one employee, one observer) and ask the manager to focus on helping the employee become aware of his or her feelings.
11. Ask two people to volunteer to role-play an employee and manager discussing a problem. Have a demonstration in front of the large group, focusing on feelings.

Designing the Workshop

There is no rule about when to stop brainstorming. You can decide to stop when you feel you have enough ideas from which to choose, or if you only have a limited amount of time in which to plan, you can decide ahead of time to limit the brainstorming to a certain number of minutes. In summary, **brainstorming is a technique that addresses the question of HOW you will implement your objectives.**

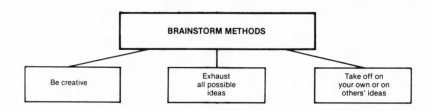

SELECTING METHODS AND STRUCTURES

The third step involved in designing is to **select the method or methods that might best achieve your goal, and the structures through which to implement these methods.** It is not always possible, however, to know ahead of time the method that will work best. It is often the case that several ideas would serve almost equally well. If you have led several workshops in a particular skill area, then you probably have an excellent sense of which methods will work most effectively. There are basically **five general categories of methods: structured experiences; non-structured experiences; lecturettes; processing; discussion.**

STRUCTURED EXPERIENCES are those **methods that have been planned ahead of time and have a particular focus.** They are structured in that each participant will have the same kind of experience, but the content will vary somewhat. In other words, the experience has been structured enough so that the participants will be involved in an experience that has the same focus, but the content of the experience will vary due to individual differences. Conducting a fantasy in which participants are asked specifically to remember a time when they felt angry is a structured experience. It has been planned ahead of time, and although each person has a different fantasy, the kind of experience each participant has will be similar. It is probably safe to assume that each person will remember a time at his/her job when he/she felt angry. The circumstances will be different; the experiencing of anger will be the same.

NON-STRUCTURED METHODS include two different levels of experiences. **In TOTAL non-structure, the group determines both the content and the structure of what is to happen.** By the eighth, ninth, or tenth session of the Supervision Skills Workshop, it might be highly appropriate not to structure all or part of the session in order to allow the participants to plan for themselves what they wish to learn. Thus, the design might include a non-structured experience—a time when the design will emerge from the group members. **In PARTIAL non-structure, the leader has determined the procedure to use, but not the content.** Often in the beginning of a workshop, we ask people to pair off and spend fifteen minutes getting to know their partners. Thus, the procedure is predetermined, but not the content of their sharing.

LECTURETTES are simply **short lectures that usually last between five and fifteen minutes,** but are sometimes longer, depending on the style of the lecturer. They generally provide a theoretical framework, or a model for the participants to use. The information given is relevant to the goals of the workshop. Lecturettes can be followed by a discussion, a question and answer period, or by structured or non-structured experiences. Again, in planning session #6, you may decide to give a lecturette on the differences between thoughts and feelings. Following that, you could decide to ask people to pair off and share their own experiences of feeling angry, sad, joyful, and afraid while at work.

DISCUSSING AND PROCESSING sometimes get equated; however, they are very different. **A discussion focuses on the content of a particular topic.** For example, if you were to introduce a discussion about the differences between thoughts and feelings, the content would be thoughts and feelings and the participants would discuss their differences. **Processing focuses on the process of the discussion, as it is happening in the present,** i.e., the dynamics. This present-ness is often referred to as "being in the here and now." The process becomes the content. Thus, if you were to process the discussion of thoughts and feelings, you would be examining such questions as:

> **How do people relate to each other in this group?**
> **Who does a lot of talking?**

Who is quiet?
Are people listening to each other?
Do some people try to enforce their views on others?

In a discussion you are concerned with WHAT people are saying; in processing you are concerned with HOW they are saying it. Both methods are useful and trainers should be familiar with them.

Knowing your audience, one of the most important elements in designing, will aid you in selecting which method(s) to use. Let us assume the group of managers have come willingly to the workshop, are eager to learn, and have been open to taking risks in the previous sessions. You may decide to use two of the above listed methods: the sentence completion exercise that asks participants to fill in the blanks, "When I feel sad, I _____," etc., and a fantasy in which they are asked to remember and to re-experience times when they felt sad, angry, joyful and afraid during work. Both ideas involve using structured experiences. The methods you choose will be very different if the managers are required to attend the workshop, are not particularly interested in learning supervision skills, and the level of risk-taking is low. In that case, you might decide to ask the participants to make lists of thoughts and feelings (a structured experience), and then you might initiate a discussion about the differences between the two. If the participants have taken some risks together, you may decide to include the sharing of work-related feelings in pairs as one of the methods. So, the more information you have about your participants, the better the position you are in to design the most appropriate workshop.

Once you have selected the methods you plan to use, you must then **determine the most appropriate structures by which the methods will be implemented.** The five possible structural arrangements are **intrapersonal, interpersonal, small group, intergroup,** and **whole group.** Sometimes the method you select dictates the structure. Other methods can be adapted to more than one structure.

INTRAPERSONAL means within the self. Intrapersonal work means the individual increases his or her awareness by himself or herself, without interaction with another person. Therefore, a method that employs an intrapersonal structure will have no dialogue or sharing of any kind among group members. There may be some sharing afterwards about what the experience was like for the participants, but essentially the participants go through the exercise alone. Intrapersonal methods include guided fantasies, meditations, art therapy, movement therapy, and written exercises. Often a guide or a facilitator is needed to lead the exercise as in certain kinds of meditations and fantasy work. Again, in planning session #6, if you choose to lead a fantasy in which participants remember and re-experience a time when they felt angry, sad, joyful, or afraid, you are using a method that assumes an intrapersonal structure. Doing the sentence completion exercise also assumes an intrapersonal structure. Often intense learning takes place intrapersonally, and the leader is unaware of the learning unless the participants choose to share it. Thus, intrapersonal methods are often powerful ways in which participants make important discoveries, but often the leader receives little immediate feedback.

INTERPERSONAL as we define it structurally in this section **means between two persons.** Any exercise that requires people to break into pairs (dyads) is utilizing an interpersonal structure. One-to-one psychotherapy is also interpersonal since it involves two people—a therapist and a client. If you choose to use the SEE-IMAGINE-FEEL exercise in session #6, you are using an interpersonal method. In this exercise participants are asked to work in pairs, taking turns making statements about what they see in their partner, what they imagine about their partner, and how they feel towards their partner. Interpersonal structures also afford much opportunity for learning, for one person is often able to facilitate another's understanding.

SMALL GROUPS are another possible structure you can use to implement methods. **Small groups range from three to five people** and provide a good opportunity for participants to give and receive feedback as well as to practice skills. Often participants in workshops try out new behaviors or skills they have learned, and working in small groups is one way they can feel relatively safe practicing these new skills. Workshops in which there is personal sharing and/or skill practicing have some degree of risk for the participants. Breaking up into small groups is a less risky way of sharing personal data and demonstrating acquired skills than practicing in front of the whole group. In planning session #6, you may decide to ask participants to break into triads (groups of three). They would then take turns role-playing manager and employee, while one of the three acts as an observer. The manager's task is to help the employee become aware of his or her feelings at work. You would then be utilizing a small group structure.

INTERGROUP METHODS means between two groups. Thus, this particular structure involves breaking one large group into two smaller groups. These two groups relate to each other at some time during the exercise. Fishbowling is an example of an intergroup activity and involves an "in" group and an "out" group. The "in" group sits in the middle of the room and performs a task, has a discussion, encounter, etc., and the "out" group members form an outside circle and function as observers. They do not participate during the exercise. When it is over the "out" group is usually asked to share its observations with the "in" group. If in planning session #6, you decide to ask two people to be employee and manager, and practice in front of the whole group, then you are using a fishbowl technique. The rest of the group sits around the two volunteers and observes, giving feedback at the end. Another example of an intergroup structure is dividing the group into two smaller groups and giving each group a separate task on which to work. At the end of the task, each group reports its learnings to the other group.

WHOLE GROUP STRUCTURES are another way to implement methods. **The group works as a whole—practicing, discussing, processing, or sharing.** If you decide to introduce a discussion on the differences between thoughts and feelings, you are using a whole group structure. If you decide to break the group into smaller groups for the same discussion, then you would be using a small group structure. Encounter groups or personal growth groups primarily use whole group structures. This type of arrangement is often used in workshops in order to process what has happened, or for the participants to do some personal sharing.

It may be clear by now that some methods dictate particular structures, while other methods would work well with more than one type of structure. A meditation is an example of a method that implies only an intrapersonal structure. A discussion about a particular topic, such as leadership skills, can utilize the following structures: interpersonal, small group, intergroup, and whole group.

One last word about methods and structures: make sure you allow the right amount of time in your design for the method(s) you have chosen. Assume you ask the participants to break into groups of three to do role plays (one manager, one employee, one observer) and practice helping the employee focus on his or her feelings. You decide to allow ten minutes of practice and ten minutes of feedback for one learning cycle. Assuming you wish to give everyone a chance to experience each role, you then need to allow one hour to complete the exercise. This kind of detailed planning is essential if you want everyone to participate equally in the experience.

Step #3 therefore answers the questions WHICH ONES (methods) and WHICH WAYS (structural arrangements) you will use to realize your goals.

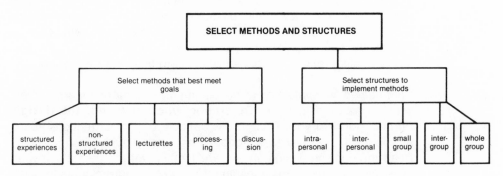

ASSESSING THE DESIGN

The fourth step in designing workshops, is to **assess the design, both objectively and subjectively,** looking at it as a whole entity, as well as looking at all of its different parts. First, **determine whether your goals are clearly stated and whether the methods you have chosen meet the goals.** For example, one of the goals in session #6 is, "The participants will learn and demonstrate interventions that help employees become aware of their feelings about their jobs," and you have chosen to use the SEE-IMAGINE-FEEL exercise (see page 43) to implement this goal. You may decide, in evaluating the design, that it is not an effective method to meet the goal, since the salient feature of the SEE-IMAGINE-FEEL exercise relates to *projecting* feelings onto others, as opposed to *experiencing* one's own feelings. A more appropriate way might be to ask the participants to break into triads (employee, manager, and observer) and role play, asking the manager to focus on helping the employee become aware of his/her feelings at work. Clearly then, many methods can be used to meet a particular goal. However, if your goal is, "The participants will become aware of how they may easily project their feelings onto their employees," then the SEE-IMAGINE-FEEL exercise would probably work very well.

The methods you choose not only need to fit the goals, but they also need to satisfy the requirements for "the elements of a good design" (see Elements). For example, if your goal is, ''The participants will learn interventions that help employees become aware of their feelings'', and you have chosen other methods in the workshop in which participants are required to break into triads, you may decide the design does not have enough variation if you again choose to use triads as a structure to meet the goal (Element #6). Therefore, you may opt for another method, perhaps conducting a fantasy in which the participants are asked to remember times when they felt angry, sad, joyful, and afraid at work, and to notice where they felt those emotions in their bodies. You may also choose to include another method, say a discussion of the differences between thoughts and feelings. The above considerations are *objective* ways to evaluate the design.

Your *subjective* evaluation of the design may be more important than your objective evaluation. **Determine whether or not the design *"feels"* good to you.** Though it is difficult to give instructions about how to tell if a design ''feels'' good, the following guidelines may help. Read through the design so you are familiar with it; then close your eyes and imagine yourself leading the workshop participants through the design. Trust any images you have. For example, if in your fantasizing you see people apparently confused, it may be that you need to simplify or change a method. Or if your design is too crowded, you may need to delete something. If in your imaginings you envision yourself very active and the participants somewhat aloof, perhaps you need to build in more ways to have fun.

If the design does ''feel'' good to you, and you are fairly convinced it will work well, ask yourself the three following questions:

"Am I comfortable with this design?"

Each trainer, no matter how skilled he or she is, feels more comfortable with some methods than with others. This statement is not an admonition to discard new methods, or ones with which you feel less comfortable. Our advice is to choose methods with which you at least feel *somewhat* comfortable, and to make sure you do feel very comfortable with most of the methods in your design. Feel free each time you lead a workshop to experiment with new methods, but limit the new methods to one or two rather than to several.

"Can I pull this off? Is it me?"

Often trainers (particularly beginners) who have attended other workshops led by dynamic trainers, have a tendency to attempt to imitate methods and style. Often the results of such imitation are disastrous. Imitating other people's styles is probably the best way *not* to develop your own. No one can really mimic another person's style; phoniness is usually apparent. Do feel free to borrow other people's methods. Just make sure you have assimilated them in your own repertoire and have a clear understanding of their use.

"Would I enjoy this design if I were a participant?"

If the answer is *no,* discover why. You probably would not want to offer a workshop to anyone in which you could not imagine being a participant.

If your answers to the above questions are *yes,* then chances are you have created an exciting, dynamic workshop for your audience, and no further revision is necessary. Thus, Step #4 addresses the question of HOW WELL your design is put together.

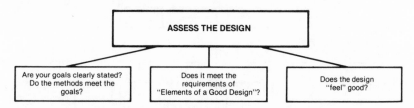

REVISING THE DESIGN

Step #5, **revision of the design,** is only to be followed if your response to any of the guidelines or questions in Step #4 is *no.* If so, you need to make some revisions in your design. After you have made the necessary revisions, again go through the assessment process until you can honestly answer *yes* to all the guidelines and questions. At that point you have completed your design.

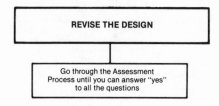

Five Easy Steps to Developing a Dynamic Design

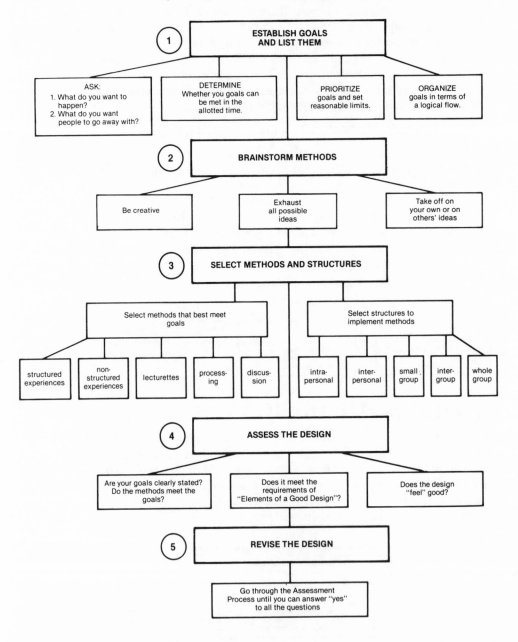

1 ESTABLISH GOALS AND LIST THEM

ASK:
1. What do you want to happen?
2. What do you want people to go away with?

DETERMINE Whether you goals can be met in the allotted time.

PRIORITIZE goals and set reasonable limits.

ORGANIZE goals in terms of a logical flow.

2 BRAINSTORM METHODS

Be creative

Exhaust all possible ideas

Take off on your own or on others' ideas

3 SELECT METHODS AND STRUCTURES

Select methods that best meet goals

Select structures to implement methods

structured experiences

non-structured experiences

lecturettes

process-ing

discus-sion

intra-personal

inter-personal

small group

inter-group

whole group

4 ASSESS THE DESIGN

Are your goals clearly stated? Do the methods meet the goals?

Does it meet the requirements of "Elements of a Good Design"?

Does the design "feel" good?

5 REVISE THE DESIGN

Go through the Assessment Process until you can answer "yes" to all the questions

CO-DESIGNING

If you are leading a workshop with another person (or persons), it is important that you design it together. This process is called co-designing, in which case the design will have emerged from both of you, and you both will be equally invested in the outcome of the workshop. The two of you will be familiar with the methods you are using and will probably feel comfortable with them. Occasionally, however, it is not possible to co-design. You may be invited (possibly as a last minute emergency measure) to co-lead a workshop that has already been designed. In this event, it is essential to completely familiarize yourself with the design. Read it carefully and translate it into words with which you feel comfortable. Make sure you understand not only the methods being used, but also the overall purpose and intention of the workshop. If you are dissatisfied with any aspects of the design, do your best to negotiate a change with your co-leader, and if possible, add some of your own ideas.

Co-designing (and subsequently co-leading) a workshop can be a rich and rewarding experience for the people involved. It can also be a painful struggle if certain considerations are ignored in the process of co-designing. This last section will identify three general areas that we feel are important to consider in order to insure that your co-designing experience is of the rich and rewarding variety. The areas discussed are: **stylistic differences, feelings,** and **responsibility.**

Differences in style are inevitable. Since no two people are exactly alike, it follows that no person's style of designing is exactly like another's. In this book, we have provided an outline that explains the design process. How people approach this process, however, will vary according to the designer(s). **It is important to take into consideration differences in ideas, thinking styles, and energy levels.**

Several years ago, one of the authors was co-designing and co-leading an eight-week workshop with three other colleagues. Because she had the most experience in teaching the subject matter she felt very insistent about doing things a certain way, and was somewhat intolerant of approaches that clashed with hers. As a result, the process of working together was filled with many struggles and much tension. Finally, one of the co-designers said to her, ''Differences are not defects.'' As these words were said, her eyes lit up, and she completely understood why they were having so much trouble designing the

Co-Designing the Workshop

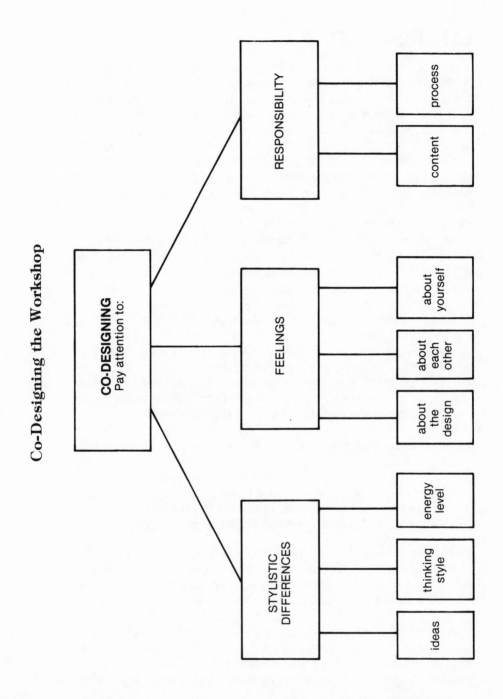

workshop. She had been viewing differences as flaws of character rather than as assets to the designing process. Her rigidity had been impeding their progress, and when she was finally able to let go of her need to "do it her own way" the process was greatly enhanced. **Consideration, therefore, needs to be given to designers' stylistic differences; we view these differences as being positive rather than negative.**

Be open to new ideas. Even if you have taught a Supervision Skills course eight times, and read all the literature available on the topic, do not reject an idea simply because you have never used it, or because you have plenty of old ideas that have worked well. Be creative with each other; bounce ideas off your co-designer. Some people get easily invested in using their own ideas. Other people relinquish their own ideas too easily in favor of their co-designer's. Therefore, trust yourself as a designer, and trust your partner. If mutual trust does not exist, then you need to find someone else with whom to design.

People have different thinking styles—another difference that needs to be considered when designing. If you and your co-designer are fortunate to have similar thinking styles by which you operate, then this area will probably not be a concern to you. Chances are, however, that they are somewhat different. Styles of thinking usually fall into **two general categories: global thinking or concrete thinking.**

People who are global thinkers generally need a substantial amount of time to familiarize themselves with the task at hand before coming up with ideas. They need to be able to talk in generalities so as to feel grounded in the subject matter, before they can set specific goals and plan ways to meet them. As global thinkers, they are usually able to generalize their learnings to different areas. In a Supervision Skills course, for example, global thinkers would probably want to extensively discuss their ideas, thoughts, or theories about supervision before beginning to design the course. People who are concrete thinkers are able to quickly generate ideas relating to goals and methods. They have little trouble being specific. For them designing is a relatively easy task, although often their designs lack some of the scope found in the designs of global thinkers.

In terms of thinking style, global thinkers tend to be slower at the designing process than concrete thinkers, but they often demonstrate a wide understanding of the overall purpose of the workshop, and as a result, their designs tend to reflect this understanding. Concrete thinkers often get impatient with global thinkers. Concrete thinkers usually want to proceed with the task of designing, and they often feel global thinkers spend too much time generalizing about concepts and ideas. On the other hand, global thinkers often get impatient with concrete thinkers, believing they are not seeing the total picture and are becoming too bogged down by details. It helps to sit down with your co-designer before even beginning to design and share with each other information about your thinking styles. Remember, the way you think influences the way you design, and the pace at which you design. **Pay attention to each other's pacing.** Differences tend to complement each other; they do not need to impede the design process.

People come to design sessions (and workshops) with varying amounts of energy—motivation, excitement, desire—with which to do their tasks. Some people almost always naturally exhibit a lot of energy. Other people come to some situations with a high amount of energy and come to others with a low amount. If you play tennis, you are aware that different players have different energy levels, and that the same individual may have more energy on one day than on another. Some tennis players enjoy playing a fast, hard game. Others prefer playing a much slower and more relaxing game. The time of day, the day's activities, and your general state of health will all influence the amount of energy you have with which to play tennis. When designing, **be open with each other in the beginning about how much energy you have to accomplish the task.** If your energy is fading, take a break, create ways to increase your energy level, or stop designing for the day. It can be a real burden to design a workshop with someone whose concerns are elsewhere.

Feelings are the second area to consider in co-designing. As people begin to work together, they develop feelings about the work they are doing, about each other, and about themselves. **It is important that co-designers explore their feelings** so that they do not unnecessarily interfere with the design process. As you continue to work, periodically ask yourself how comfortable you are with the subject matter, how you are feeling about your partner, about yourself, and about the design process.

If you are designing a Sexuality Workshop for male and female nursing students, it is important to be aware of your feelings about the topic so they will not unconsciously interfere with the designing process. You may discover that you do not feel very comfortable talking about homosexuality, but if your partner does, then allow him or her to lead that portion of the workshop. You may wish to share your uncomfortable feelings with the participants. They will probably sense them anyway, and your self-disclosure will be important role-modeling behavior. If this is one of your first attempts at designing and leading a workshop on sexuality, you may feel somewhat uncomfortable about your lack of experience in that area; or you may feel you have less to contribute than your co-designer. If so, acknowledge your feelings to your partner. You will not be able to change the reality of the situation, but chances are you will feel more comfortable once you have stated your feelings, and be better able to do your job.

No matter how considerate you are towards your co-designer, it is almost inevitable that from time to time you will experience negative feelings towards each other. These negative feelings, if discussed openly, need not be obstacles to the design process. Instead, they can be learning experiences from which you gain insight into some aspect of your behavior. One of the authors remembers co-designing with a friend and feeling angry at her for constantly interrupting the process to make phone calls. She imagined the workshop must not be important to her co-designer, so she decided she would not get too invested in the process either. Finally, they each became aware of what was happening and were able to discuss their feelings, make some adjustments in their work together, and get a better understanding of each of their behaviors.

Certain kinds of negative feelings may emerge more than others. If your partner is contributing more, or is seemingly more involved in the process than you are, then your partner may begin to feel some anger towards you. Or perhaps feeling angry at yourself, you may project these feelings onto your co-designer. Feelings of disappointment about the design may also develop. One of you may not like, or may not agree with many of your partner's ideas. You may find yourself arguing about which methods to select. You may be unable to reach an agreement that feels good to both of you. One or both of you may begin to feel bored with the topic. These and other kinds of negative feelings may emerge from time to time. There is no magical solution to make them disappear. What is essential, however, is that you express the negative feelings to each other. This open expression does not necessarily make the negative feelings go away, but it often enables you to put them aside and continue on, despite them, in a more productive way. Or, perhaps you can negotiate some changes or make some compromises that will enable you both to feel more satisfied.

We believe that the process of designing is usually fun, exciting, and challenging for the people involved. Co-designers usually experience many positive feelings that are rewarding and that facilitate the designing process. Occasionally, however, too much excitement can interfere if you get so caught up in your excitement that you lose perspective of the workshop. For example, one of the authors was teaching a ten-week Basic Counseling Skills course for people who had little experience in counseling. She was involved on her own in a more advanced clinical training program in which she learned many new techniques. Because she was so excited about these new techniques, she decided to teach some of them to her students. It became apparent in the midst of the course, that her decision was inappropriate. The students had a difficult time understanding the techniques, probably because they did not have enough of a foundation in the basic skills. If she had had a better overall perspective of the goals of the course, and if her enthusiasm had not clouded her vision, this mistake could have been avoided.

If you are designing with someone who has had much more experience in leading workshops than you have, or has had more experience in leading workshops on the assigned topic, then it is easy to feel inferior to your partner and lose sight of your own skills. Give yourself some gentle reassurance. It is rare that two (or more) people co-designing will have the same skill levels; differences in competency are okay. Your partner can still learn from you. There is no rule in co-designing that says each of you has to contribute fifty percent of the ideas.

Responsibility—how the work will be shared in the actual workshop—is the final area you need to consider in co-designing. Once your design is completed, it is important to decide who will be responsible for what parts of the workshop. There are **two categories of responsibility: responsibility for content and responsibility for process.** The latter will be discussed in the section on leadership. Remember that content relates to the subject matter of the workshop. Process refers to the group dynamics. For the current discussion, we will refer only to responsibility as it pertains to content.

First, you need to **decide how leadership will be shared.** Are you co-leaders, or is one person an assistant leader, in which case he or she will probably take less responsibility for leading the workshop. If one of you is an assistant leader then be clear with each other how much less responsibility the assistant will be assuming. You need to address the following questions:

Will the assistant leader be introducing any ideas or methods?
How much freedom will he or she have to make interventions related to the content?
If you are co-leaders, who will take responsibility for introducing different aspects of the workshop design?

It is often helpful to share the different leadership functions pertaining to the design. For example, for the first part of the workshop one of you can introduce the didactic portion, and the other can introduce the experiential part. Then you can switch responsibilities during the next part of the workshop.

It is important also, to **decide ahead of time, how much freedom each of you will have to make any changes in the design.** You may discover the workshop is taking more time than you had planned, and you may need to make some last minute deletions. On the other hand, the workshop may be progressing more quickly than you had imagined, and you may want to add something, or allow more time for some of the exercises you had planned. Decide ahead of time if you are willing to have either one of you make last minute changes, or whether you want to discuss any changes together in the midst of the group. Determine beforehand if it will be acceptable to have your co-leader present additional thoughts, or give further directions to the segment for which you are responsible. This kind of careful planning usually avoids any misunderstanding or negative feelings that may develop between co-leaders.

Most likely, as mentioned under *feelings,* one of you will have more expertise in a particular area than another. If you are co-leaders, do not assume the person with the most experience should take the most responsibility for leading the workshop. Or if one of you is more familiar with a certain method do not assume the person with the most familiarity leads that particular section. Making these assumptions is an excellent way *not* to increase your leadership skills. **The best way**

to expand your skill level is by practicing, not by observing someone else. Observation does help, but just observing limits the opportunities to develop your expertise. Respect each other's strengths and limitations. It is okay to be a beginner!

LEADING THE WORKSHOP 3

So far we have been concerned with how to prepare for a workshop and how to create a successful design. How the workshop design is transmitted to the participants is the subject of the third section of this book. Much of the quality and flavor of a delicious meal is lost if it is not served properly. The same is true of a workshop. An excellent design does not guarantee a successful workshop unless it is led skillfully. In Part Three we hope to convey information that will enable group leaders to increase their skills in leading workshops. We discuss some of the key issues involved in being an effective group leader/teacher/trainer. We discuss the qualities and behaviors of a good leader, leadership styles, leadership functions, levels of intervention, the management of difficult behaviors, and co-leading issues. An understanding of all these aspects of leadership is essential in order to develop into a skillful group leader. It is important to remember, however, that there is no substitute for practice. The more you practice, the better leader you will become. Following the steps involved in designing, as well as understanding and applying the leadership skills we outline, will greatly enhance the workshops you design and lead.

QUALITIES OF AN EFFECTIVE LEADER

Leadership talent is often thought to be something an individual either does or does not possess. Probably all of us have heard the expression he or she is ''a born leader.'' Implicit in this quotation is the notion that a person is either a good leader or not a good leader, and that one's classification in terms of leadership cannot be reversed. This section will hopefully dispel that myth. Although we believe there are specific qualities and behaviors that differentiate effective leaders from ineffective ones, we believe that these qualities and behaviors can be acquired and demonstrated. If each of us were to brainstorm a list of the qualities of a good leader, each list would probably be quite extensive. We could come up with a myriad of positive adjectives that comprise a list entitled "ideal leader." In this section we have chosen to discuss ten qualities we believe are especially important to possess if one is to be an effective leader. Our list is not exhaustive; you may choose to add additional qualities. In this chapter we will explain ways to translate these qualities into specific behaviors and kinds of interventions.

ACTIVE LISTENING is the first quality of a good leader. This term refers to **the ability to hear not only what a person is stating, but**

Qualities of an Effective Leader

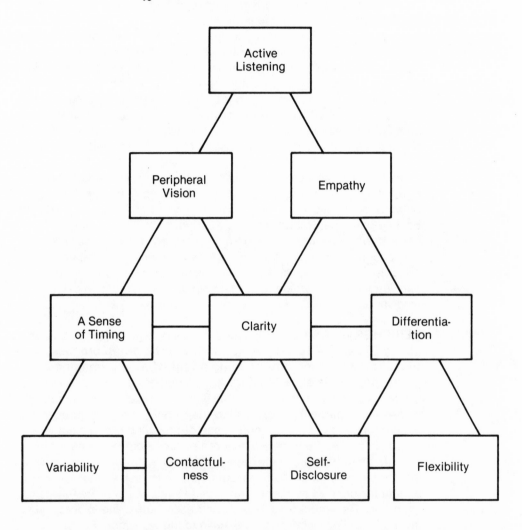

also what his or her underlying feelings are about the subject. Active listening means being able to hear a person's statement in a wide context, that is, understanding the feelings, thoughts, and concerns that surround the person's words. Dr. Theodore Reik, a well known psychoanalyst, calls this process "listening with the third ear." The third ear hears material that is not explicitly said, but which is of crucial importance, and that the person may not even consciously

Leading the Workshop

acknowledge. One of the authors was recently engaged in an initial counseling session with a young woman who was the client. The latter was talking about how people often do not seem to understand what she says, and this situation is upsetting to her. Since the author (counselor) was "listening with her third ear," she thought the client might also be wondering (1) if there was something wrong with her, and (2) if the counselor was able to understand her. The counselor then fed back to the client the concerns she heard by listening with her third ear. The client found this information quite helpful, for she was indeed afraid there was something terribly disturbing about herself, and she wondered if the counselor would really be able to understand her.

Often in workshops, participants do not express their feelings and concerns directly. They may be afraid to share them or they may not even be consciously aware of them. Listening with a third ear, and feeding back to participants what you are hearing, helps them feel heard and understood. This allows them to feel supported and to be more open to subsequent learnings. It is not always necessary or appropriate, however, to reflect back everything you hear with your "third ear." The leader must decide what is helpful within the context of the workshop.

PERIPHERAL VISION is a second quality of a good leader. It is **the ability to sense—to see, hear, and intuit the group process, and to make a fairly accurate reading about what you imagine each group member is experiencing.** A good leader attempts to be aware of what is going on in the group at all times. Although he or she may be addressing a particular individual, or delivering a short lecturette, the leader needs to have a general sense of how all the participants are responding. If some people are bored or tuned out, it is important to have that information, as the leader will probably want to find a way to include them. If the leader senses someone is feeling angry, it is important to notice what effect, if any, these angry feelings are having on the group. The leader then needs to assess whether the expression of the angry feelings would be productive to the workshop. Peripheral vision is a quality that takes some practice to acquire. It is impossible to know, with one hundred percent accuracy and without checking out your assumptions, what each person is experiencing, but the more accurate you are, the more likely you are to exercise your leadership effectively. Acquiring peripheral vision involves tuning into people's body cues—postures, facial expressions, gestures, etc. that give some indication of how that person is feeling. It involves listening to the quality of feeling in people's voices, sensing the atmosphere in the room, and watching how people relate to each other.

EMPATHY is a third quality of a good leader. This term refers to **the ability to put oneself "in the other person's shoes," to see the world as he or she sees it.** Every person's beliefs, values, feelings, outlooks on life, etc., are influenced by his or her unique experiences. No two people see things exactly alike. An effective leader is able to imagine what the world looks like from another's eyes, or to coin a popular colloquial expression, "understand where that person is coming from." Since no two people think or experience life exactly alike, it follows that different people have different needs. An empathic leader is able to respond appropriately to various individual needs. In a given workshop some participants may be much more familiar with the material than others; participants are also at different levels in their knowledge of and experience with the subject matter, and in their awareness of their own dynamics. Therefore, an empathic leader recognizes these differences, has different expectations for different members, and responds to group members according to their particular needs.

SENSE OF TIMING is another important quality of an effective trainer. **Good timing means knowing when to intervene and when to remain silent.** Often trainers find themselves taking up too much air time—making too many interventions and taking too long to make them. Sometimes it is best not to overwork an idea or an issue. Often silences are a wonderful way for people to absorb information or experience feelings. Silences can seem awkward at times, particularly to beginning trainers, but it is important to remember their usefulness. Having a good sense of timing involves being able to evaluate the mood of the group as well as the mood of individuals in the group. Too many interventions from the trainer often leave group members feeling bombarded. As a result, they lose much of the cognitive as well as the emotional impact of the workshop. Trainers who intervene too little, or at inappropriate times, probably are not getting across effectively the material they wish to present. Inappropriate interventions tend to stop the flow of the group. Members often become confused and quiet when the leader's comments seem inappropriate.

CLARITY is a fifth quality of an effective leader. Since we are talking about learning experiences, the group members will probably be attending the workshop for the primary purpose of learning new material, either theory or skills. It is important that the trainer **convey information in a way that is succinct and easy to understand.** Material that is confusing and/or tedious in nature usually gets lost rather than absorbed. Trainers who are able to be clear and to the point usually hold the attention of the participants, particularly if the content is interesting. It is therefore important for trainers to be highly familiar with their material so they can convey it simply to others.

DIFFERENTIATION is a sixth quality of a good leader. It is **the ability of the trainer to separate him/herself from the participants, so that he or she is able to facilitate the group process rather than to become enmeshed with it.** A group leader needs to have a reasonable amount of awareness of his or her own personality characteristics, defenses, and styles of behavior, otherwise they may unwittingly be projected onto group members. It is a common mistake for group leaders as well as group members to attribute their own hostility, anger, or other feelings to another person. One of these authors remembers leading a group in which she began to feel quite angry towards one of the group members for continually disagreeing with what was said. Instead of recognizing these feelings in herself, and either confronting the person or choosing to ignore his expressed negativity, she suggested that perhaps other people were annoyed with his behavior. As it turned out, this member's behavior seemed to bother the leader much more than anyone else. Projecting feelings onto group members usually contributes to mistrust of the leader. Often group members begin to feel unsafe in terms of taking risks, asking questions, and stating their feelings. As a result, they often withdraw or become less open. Thus, differentiation refers to the ability to distinguish between one's own thoughts and feelings, and those of others.

VARIABILITY is a seventh quality of a good leader. Variability means **the ability to be both confrontative and supportive, serious or light, depending on the circumstances.** Participants in a workshop need to be supported and encouraged to explore new ideas or try out new skills. Occasionally a group member needs to be confronted by the leader, particularly if his or her behavior is disruptive and is negatively affecting the others. Sometimes people's assumptions or statements need to be challenged, and if the trainer can do so in a caring, rather than in an accusatory way, the group members will probably be receptive rather than defensive. People often express important and deep feelings in workshops. It is essential that the leader respect these feelings or group members will quickly begin to hide their emotions. It is equally important that leaders develop and use their sense of humor. Laughter almost always makes an experience more enjoyable, and enjoyment is an aid to learning. The ability to laugh at oneself is a good way to gain new perspectives on one's behavior. People who can laugh at their mistakes, shortcomings, and behavioral patterns are generally open to change and learning.

CONTACTFULNESS is an eighth important leader quality. The contactful leader has **the ability to reach each person, to touch each member emotionally, intellectually, or physically.** The contactful leader is truly involved in the group experience. The whole self—the emotional, physical, intellectual, and spiritual parts are present, and the leader makes no attempt to hide or close off these parts. A leader who is contactful is not afraid of other people's emotions, and does not withdraw when group members express vulnerability. Rather he or she is emotionally available to support and encourage people to express themselves and to take risks. Contact involves a meeting of minds, spirits, and/or emotions, and effective leaders make a great deal of contact with group members, while encouraging the latter to make contact with each other.

SELF-DISCLOSURE is a ninth quality we have identified as being important. Effective leaders are able to be distant enough from the group so as to maintain their perspective. At the same time, however, they are genuinely self-disclosing and allow themselves to be seen as a "real person." Self-disclosure means **a willingness to share one's feelings, thoughts, reactions, and appropriate personal information with group members.** We do not mean to imply it is necessary to share intimate details of one's personal life. That kind of self-disclosure is neither necessary nor appropriate. A leader who is self-disclosing, however, is not afraid to acknowledge nervousness about the workshop, or any other feelings he or she experiences during the course of the workshop. The leader feels comfortable with his or her strengths as well as vulnerabilities. If a leader is open and self-disclosing, he or she sets the tone for the workshop and usually the group members will feel more comfortable disclosing themselves.

FLEXIBILITY is the final quality we have identified in this section. An effective leader comes in with a design and a structure for the workshop. He or she has some preconceived notions about the nature of the participants and some ideas of what it will be like working with them. The leader's approach is influenced by how he or she imagines the group members will respond. An effective leader, however, is **willing to give up these preconceptions and make changes in the design if necessary.** If the content or the structure is not meeting the needs of the participants, and they are not responding positively, then it is important to make some changes.

In order to make an appropriate change the trainer needs to diagnose the problem. It could be the content is unclear, too elementary, or uninteresting. Perhaps the structures are inappropriate for the group. For example, the participants may be intimidated by experiential methods; they may need to gradually build up trust before agreeing to take part in an experiential exercise. Perhaps a lecturette is too long or boring, and a discussion would be more interesting. The trainer needs to periodically ask group members how they are feeling about the workshop. Usually, however, when participants are responding negatively, the trainer (as well as group members) can "feel it in the air." The trainer can ask members directly what kinds of changes they would like to see. Although it is essential to be flexible, the trainer is there because he or she has some expertise in the subject. Therefore, the trainer should have the final say about what changes he or she is willing to incorporate. It is okay to decide not to make all the changes that participants request. What is important is that you listen to their suggestions and then make decisions based on the best interests of everyone involved.

We have now identified and defined **ten qualities** we feel are highly **important in an effective leader.** They are: **ACTIVE LISTENING, PERIPHERAL VISION, EMPATHY, TIMING, CLARITY, DIFFEREN-TIATION, VARIABILITY, CONTACTFULNESS, SELF-DISCLOSURE, and FLEXIBILITY.** No leader possesses or displays one hundred percent of each of these qualities. What is crucial is that, as leaders, we are aware of their importance, and strive to exhibit them in our behavior as much as possible. A few forms for periodic self-evaluation with relation to these ten qualities are presented in Appendix D. As leaders/trainers/teachers, we must expect of ourselves what we expect of our participants—the willingness to learn, to grow, and to change.

EFFECTIVE TRAINER BEHAVIORS

A trainer serves as a role model for participants. They learn not only from what is said directly, but also from how the trainer conducts the workshop. **It is essential that the leader's behavior be congruent with what he or she is teaching.** For example, if you are offering a Communication Skills Workshop and have trouble expressing yourself clearly, you will lack credibility as a teacher. If you are giving a lecturette on the importance of expressing feelings, and you have remained distant from your participants, and have not expressed feelings during the workshop, you lose significant impact. We have identified some behaviors that are necessary to be an effective trainer.

Effective Trainer Behaviors

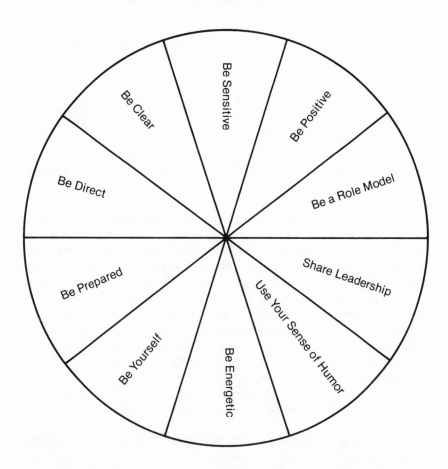

The first is to **be prepared.** In order to offer a workshop in a specialized field you need to know the subject matter you are teaching.

Preparation can include research, actual designing, and practicing your presentation. With beginning designers it is helpful to practice aloud, giving directions and presenting the lecturettes. Make a tape recording of yourself while practicing; this enables you to evaluate your style of presentation and/or the content of the material. If you are having difficulty with a part of the design, be sure to work out any problems before the workshop. Sometimes trainers dismiss these difficulties and hope everything will turn out all right; this assumption often produces unnecessary anxiety. Take the time to fully prepare yourself for the workshop. It is the best way to feel secure and pleased with your design.

The second effective trainer behavior is to **be yourself—nobody can be you better than you.** If you have participated in several workshops you may be tempted to imitate trainers you liked. Trying to copy someone else's style can cause problems. Instead, identify what you specifically like about an individual trainer's style and incorporate that quality in a manner that fits you. Do not use language that is not comfortable for you. Phrases used easily by one person can sound awkward or phony when imitated. Trust that with adequate preparation and learning from others you can develop an effective style that is most natural for you and therefore most exciting for the participants.

The third effective trainer behavior is to **be energetic.** As the trainer, you set the climate and tone of the workshop. Initially, you provide the motivation and excitement for learning. **Only when you are excited about what you are doing can you communicate that excitement to participants.** A few ways to share your energy and excitement with participants are to make eye contact, speak loudly and clearly, vary your voice in tempo and pitch, and use gestures when you speak. In addition, encourage others to speak so everyone can hear. If you notice people's attention waning, change the tone of your voice and/or provide an exercise that involves physical movement. Movement allows for an expansion of people's energy. Sitting and talking for long periods of time often invites fatigue. Therefore, vary the activities in order to maintain an energetic learning environment.

The fourth effective trainer behavior is to **use your sense of humor.** As stated earlier, learning can be fun if you make it fun. One of the best ways to have a workshop that is fun is to **encourage humor whenever possible.** Humorous examples help participants to relax and provide a sense of group unity. Often an idea or concept can best be explained by using humor. A witty anecdote can highlight an idea in a poignant way. In addition, we believe humor describes the human experience in a way that allows people to take themselves less seriously without discounting their experience. Participants may place too much pressure on themselves, thereby getting in the way of the learning process. Humor provides both trainer and participants with another way of viewing themselves that is meaningful, fun, and creative.

The fifth effective trainer behavior is to **be direct—when you have something to say, say it as honestly and as straightforwardly as possible.** For example, if you are feeling bored, share that feeling with the participants. Feeling uncomfortable and "beating around the bush" will not alleviate your discomfort. The participants will know when you are being less than honest. It is difficult to hide strong feelings. If you are direct with participants, you encourage them by your behavior to be direct with you and with each other. If you tend to "beat around the bush" you may find others doing the same. Therefore, the more honest and direct you are as a trainer, the more you serve as a positive role-model for participants.

The sixth effective trainer behavior is to **be clear.** Earlier we discussed the importance of knowing your subject matter. It is also necessary to present the subject matter clearly. **Eliminate confusion and ambiguity** so that what you say is easily grasped and understood. If you have to re-explain a concept several times, your presentation is probably unclear. Some of the best ideas are lost when the trainer has difficulty explaining them easily. Being clear is a skill that can be easily practiced by listening to yourself.

The seventh effective trainer behavior is to **be sensitive to participants.** By gathering information about the participants and incorporating some of the values of humanistic learning into your design, you are already demonstrating sensitivity. During the workshop, maintain your sensitivity to members' needs. As a trainer, **periodically ask participants how they are feeling.** Paying attention to people's feelings and being responsive to their changing needs are additional ways of being sensitive. Although being goal-directed is essential in a designed workshop experience, doing so at the expense of the learners' feelings or needs is counterproductive. Therefore, an effective trainer is capable of both being sensitive to participants as well as working towards reaching the goals of the workshop.

The eighth effective trainer behavior we discuss is **sharing leadership with the participants.** When the workshop begins, you are the designated leader. As the workshop progresses, you can share leadership with participants. Shared leadership produces greater involvement and investment from the group members. Group members exercising leadership is usually a sign of further commitment to the group. You do not have to stay "in charge" if there are others willing and capable of assuming leadership. **Sharing leadership means participants may lead discussions, teach, add examples from personal experience, and initiate the processing and evaluation of the workshop.** There is room for several people to assume responsibility for the workshop. In creating an environment that allows participants to use their leadership skills, you are exhibiting one of the most important leadership traits: the willingness to share power.

The ninth effective trainer behavior is to **be a role-model.** Being a leader means you are in a powerful position and your behavior is likely to influence others. If the participants feel positively towards you, they will most likely try to emulate some of your behavior. Therefore, **behave in ways that are consistent with your value system,** and group members will probably behave in similar ways. Taking risks is an example of a behavior that is desirable to see evidenced in groups. If you take risks, the participants will probably do likewise. Risk-taking behavior includes showing vulnerabilities with group members, practicing new skills, or encouraging feedback about yourself or about the group. Although taking risks can be somewhat scary, it is a wonderful way to grow personally, to increase your self-awareness, and to improve skills. It is important to remember that your behavior is being watched and that in many ways you are a model for participants.

The last effective trainer behavior is to **be positive.** By this term we mean optimistic, supportive, and encouraging. As a trainer, **it is essential that you believe in people's unlimited potential to grow and change in a positive direction.** As discussed in the overview, the kinds of expectations teachers have about students affects the way the students feel about themselves, and the rate at which they learn. Feeling positive, as well as acting positively, conveys the message that what you have to teach is exciting, interesting, and important, and that the students, too, will be able to learn and grow personally as well as professionally. It is important to be positive about making mistakes. A former teacher of the authors claims that if you learn from a mistake, it is then transformed into knowledge and becomes a learning experience. Anything that goes "wrong" in a workshop can be a valuable learning experience, as long as your attitude is positive and you are willing to learn from the experience.

LEADERSHIP STYLES

We define **three basic leadership styles** that, we believe, form the basis for all leadership styles: **authoritarian, democratic, and shared.** Although we will discuss each of them separately, we do not wish to give the impression that each exists in a vacuum, unrelated to the others. In our experience leaders tend to assume primarily one of the three basic styles, while incorporating some of the other three leadership styles into their particular approach. Each style has its advantages and disadvantages, which we identify. Some styles we believe are more appropriate most of the time than others. For the sake of clarity we are presenting each style of leadership in its extreme form, as if it is not in any way influenced by the others.

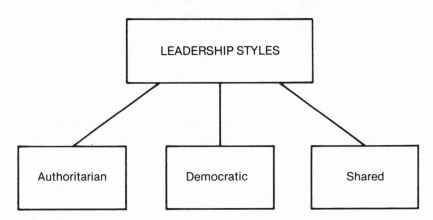

THE AUTHORITARIAN LEADER is one who makes all of the group's decisions. This type of leader assumes control of the procedures and activities. Members are either told explicitly not to quarrel with the leader, or else that message becomes implicit in the way the leader responds to group members. The norm is thus established not to challenge the leader. An authoritarian leader maintains emotional distance from group members. He or she does not express feelings within the group and does not share personal experiences. He or she remains apart from the group by acting only as a teacher, information giver, or observer.

This style of leadership is generally ineffective. Group members often feel manipulated into participating in activities. They can also feel resentful about adhering to rules and procedures with which they do not agree and in which they have no say. As a result, group members often begin to feel angry at the group leader, yet they are afraid to express their anger directly. Unexpressed anger can often manifest itself indirectly in negative attitudes, sarcasm, emotional withdrawal, or in countless other ways. In addition, authoritarian leaders seem to frequently squelch ideas and suggestions offered by group members. New ideas are often seen as a challenge to their authoritarian leadership. Therefore, group members have little or no say in making decisions. These behaviors of the authoritarian leader frequently contribute to group members having a low investment in the group. Thus this leadership style seems to limit participants' receptivity, participation, and creativity.

There are occasions when an authoritarian style is necessary and appropriate. One instance is when the leader has a limited time to convey the material, and for the sake of expediency, he or she makes the decisions and sets the rules. One of the authors remembers an instance in which she needed to assume this style of leadership. Several years ago, she worked in a counseling program with ex-offenders. As part of her job she led Employability Development Workshops for inmates who were almost ready to be released from prison. Since these men and women were accustomed to being controlled most of the day by prison officials, they were determined to test their behavioral limits with the group leader. Since their attitude toward prison was quite negative, they generalized this attitude to most activities offered within the prison, including the Employability Development Workshops.

In this situation it was important for the leader to set firm rules, particularly in the beginning of the workshop, and to make it clear disruptive behavior would not be tolerated. Otherwise the climate might be such that no learning could take place. As group members discovered the leader's consistency in setting the limits, her sincerity in wanting to teach, and her belief in the subject matter, they became more responsive within the group. In turn, the leader was able to be less controlling and allow others to take on some of the leadership functions she had been assuming. Thus the leader's authoritarian style was appropriate in the initial stage of the group, in order for her to be able to present the material, and ensure the success of the workshop.

As in the above example, you may sometimes initially exhibit leadership behaviors of an authoritarian style. Later you may change your style as the group is able to appropriately share in the decision-making process.

A DEMOCRATIC LEADER is one who allows group members to have a voice and a vote in decision-making. He or she is primarily responsible for deciding what material will be taught and how it will be presented. The leader is also responsible for managing the group process so as to ensure the smooth functioning of the group. The group members, however, are able to influence and vote on such issues as starting and ending times, breaks, time limits, and occasionally (particularly in longer workshops) on the content. Members are free to participate or not participate in exercises. Group members are encouraged to assume leadership roles, both content and process functions. (See "Leadership Functions".) A democratic leader respects differences of opinion. He or she allows group members to disagree freely with his or her ideas, while encouraging members to express their own ideas. Expressing opinions different from the leader is seen as constructive thinking rather than as a challenge. A democratic leader is emotionally available to group members. He or she shares feelings when appropriate, and relates personal experiences in the context of the material being presented. He or she is not afraid of becoming involved in the group and is not afraid of being vulnerable.

A democratic leadership style is almost always effective. Group members feel respected and valued. They are encouraged to think for themselves and to challenge ideas or rules with which they disagree. Their investment in the outcome of the group is high because they are allowed to participate in the decision-making process and to freely express their thoughts and opinions. Group members readily generate ideas since their creativity is encouraged. In general, group members respond warmly and positively to democratic group leaders, and in turn, they respond positively to the workshop as a whole.

There are occasions, however, when democratic leadership is not effective. If the time for the workshop is limited, and the leader is concerned about presenting a lot of material in a small amount of time, it is not helpful to use precious time asking members to vote on decisions the leader could be making. There may be instances too, when group members who were outvoted feel resentful that they did not get what they wanted, or that everyone did not agree on the decision.

Although voting is often a useful way to come to a decision, it can also suppress conflicts in the group that might otherwise be resolved by a lengthier discussion designed to reach consensus.

SHARED LEADERSHIP pertains to a situation in which **there is a designated leader, but all the group decisions as well as the leadership functions are shared by the group members.** The leader's opinions have just as much influence as each of the member's opinions. The responsibility for the content of the workshop may be shared, for although leadership is determined, it can change. All participants are equally responsible for the group process. Therefore, different members at different times exhibit leadership roles. The designated leader is emotionally available to the group. He or she shares feelings and personal experiences. There is no more separation or distance between the leader and the group members than there is among the group members themselves. Decisions are usually made by consensus. Issues are decided by group members voicing their ideas, feelings, and opinions, until all members agree to a particular decision.

This type of leadership is effective when group members demonstrate leadership skills and when members have a high investment in the group. In order for shared leadership to work there has to be a commitment from the group members to each other and to the group process. The participants must want to cultivate their leadership skills and be willing to practice them. With this style of leadership, participants feel valued and respected. They readily generate ideas, for ideas are encouraged. Group members get practice being leaders and they learn to assume more responsibility in groups.

Shared leadership tends to be ineffective in most workshop situations. Participants do not usually have the skill level or the investment in the group to assume the responsibility of a leader. Reaching consensus tends to be more time-consuming than voting. When all members are responsible for the group process, it usually gets much attention and takes up a large amount of the group's time. In most workshops time is limited, and although the group process is important, it cannot assume a major role.

The following instance describes a workshop situation in which a shared leadership style was extremely effective. One of the authors participated in a ten-day workshop called "Training for Trainers." As you can probably guess, the purpose of the workshop was to train the participants to become more skilled leaders/trainers. During the first half of the training the designated leader primarily assumed a democratic leadership style, while effectively role-modeling the functions of a good leader. During the second half of the workshop, however, the leadership was shared. Participants took turns being the designated leader, and they were expected throughout the workshop to assume leadership functions and to be responsible for the group process. As you can probably imagine, this shared leadership style facilitated the development of leadership skills among the workshop participants.

In determining what your primary leadership style will be, it is important to assess the nature as well as the skill level of the participants. You also need to be aware of the length of the workshop. You can then choose the leadership style with which you feel most comfortable, and that is most appropriate.

LEVELS OF INTERVENTION

If you have ever participated in or led a group, then you are aware that there are different ways in which the group leader(s) can address participants. Sometimes the leader speaks directly to an individual, sometimes he or she speaks only to some members of the group , and at other times the leader addresses the group as a whole. We call these **three ways of addressing group members** levels of interventions. Level one is the **individual level,** level two is the **interpersonal level,** and level three is the **group level.** We will discuss each of them.

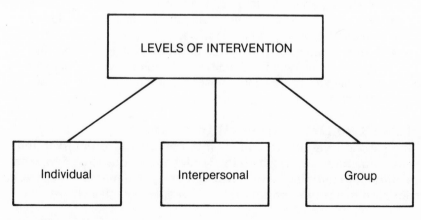

Level One (Individual) Intervention

When a leader is making an intervention on the individual level, he or she is asking a question of, or making a statement to one particular member of the group. A leader may choose to intervene at this level in different circumstances. Perhaps the individual is focusing attention to himself or herself by making a statement or by asking a question, and as leader, you respond directly to that person. Or you may choose to use a particular individual as an example to help you highlight a point. You may ask that individual if he or she is willing to participate in an experiment or to demonstrate a skill or behavior. You might also decide it would be helpful to a particular individual if you addressed him or her directly, in order to give support, or to help him or her gain further understanding of an idea. Finally, you may want to draw attention to an individual whose behavior is being particularly disruptive in an effort to eliminate the behavior.

When intervening on the individual level you are drawing attention to a particular person. Level one interventions are quite focused and direct. A level one intervention also gives the individual recognition and attention which may or may not have a positive effect. Some group members may find this attention supportive and helpful; others may feel uncomfortable being the center of attention. Therefore, it is important to be positive and reassuring so the individual does not feel that he or she is being openly criticized. The following are examples of level one (individual) interventions:

- ''Nancy, I really appreciate your volunteering for the exercise. You took a big risk.''
- ''In answer to your question, Steve, I wonder if you would be willing to participate in an experiment?''
- ''Michael, it may be helpful if you approached the solution to the problem with this idea in mind.''
- ''Jane, I am having a lot of difficulty getting through the material when you continually ask me questions. Would you be willing to reserve your questions for the end of the presentation?''

Level Two (Interpersonal) Intervention

The second level of intervention, **interpersonal level intervention, refers to situations in which the leader asks a question or makes a statement directed toward two or more group members, but not directed toward the entire group.** As leader, you may choose to intervene at the interpersonal level in various circumstances. It is possible that two or more people are involved in an interesting experience and you want the whole group to be aware of what is going on. Or an issue may arise in the group that you want to highlight, involving how a few participants are relating to one another. The ways in which the participants are interacting may be positive or negative. You may want to ask two participants you noticed working well together to discuss their style of problem solving. Or, you may ask those individuals who seem to be in conflict with one another to take the time to resolve their differences. Their method of conflict resolution may be a useful example for other group members.

When intervening on the interpersonal level you are highlighting the dynamics of two, or of a few individuals involved in the group. This level of intervention is quite direct and focused, although the focus is on more than one person. Since the attention is being shared, however, it is unlikely either person will feel self-conscious. Following are some interpersonal examples of level two interventions:

- "Jane and John, would you describe to the rest of the group what it was like for the two of you to work together? What techniques did you use to solve the problem?"
- "Sandra, Paul, and Alan, you seem to be unable to resolve your differences. Let's take a moment to discover what your conflict is all about."
- "Joel and Sarah, you were discussing an interesting issue a few moments ago. Would you tell the rest of the group about it?"

Level Three (Group) Intervention

The third level of intervention, the **group level, is used in situations in which the leader is asking a question or making a statement directed to the group as a whole.** A leader may choose to intervene at the group level under various circumstances. A level three intervention is highly appropriate when the leader does not want to place the responsibility for a response on any one individual. The intervention may be specific in its content, but it is directed to the entire group. Sometimes in a group, one member is acting in a disruptive manner, but the leader may be reluctant to address the individual personally. An intervention directed at the group will hopefully "reach" the guilty party. Therefore it is occasionally appropriate to use group level interventions as a way of giving feedback to an individual who might respond negatively to feedback directed at him or her alone.

A level three intervention puts no one on the spot. Everyone is included and the leader asks the group to share in the responsibility of reacting. A group intervention is significantly less direct than the other two interventions and is therefore less confronting. Following are some examples of level three (group) interventions:

- "Several suggestions have been made; which one would you like to discuss first?"
- "How did you all feel about the slide presentation?"
- "I noticed people became quiet after John talked about the difficulties he is having as a new manager. Why do you think that was so?"
- "We have heard from a couple of people quite frequently. What do you think the rest of you think?"
- "Let's try to give everyone an opportunity to speak."

As leader you can intervene at any one of these three levels—individual, interpersonal, and group. If you notice that you primarily intervene on the individual or interpersonal level, you may want to practice interventions that are more general and less confronting. If you primarily or exclusively intervene on the group level, you may want to experiment with interventions that are more direct and confronting. What is critical to remember is that each intervention will affect the group in a different way. Therefore, select those levels of intervention that are most appropriate in your particular workshop.

LEADERSHIP FUNCTIONS

The group leader determines the goals of the workshop as well as the methods used to implement them. Therefore, the leader is primarily responsible for organizing and directing the workshop in such a manner that the goals of the workshop, are met. In order to meet these goals and create a successful workshop, the leader must exhibit two primary functions. We call these: **content functions** and **process functions.**

The leader has expertise in a given area, and his or her responsibility is to present information that will provide both theory and new skills to participants. When the leader is providing information and demonstrating skills, he or she is exhibiting a content function. When the leader is behaving in such a way as to facilitate the interactions, behaviors, and feelings of the participants, he or she is demonstrating a process function. Therefore, when the leader is presenting a model

Leadership Functions

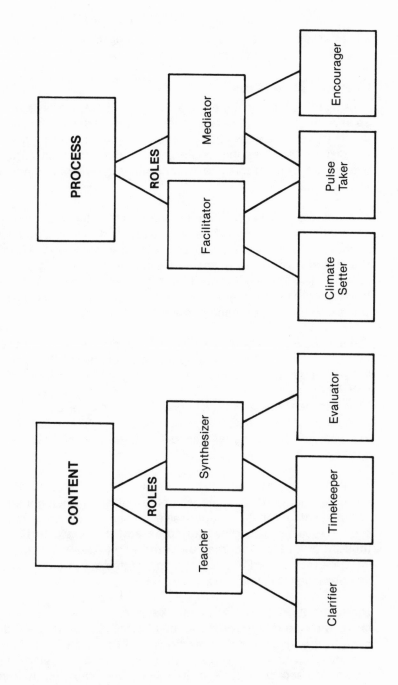

of interviewing, this is a demonstration of a content function. When a leader asks participants to express their feelings about the workshop, he or she is demonstrating a process function.

Content Functions

Looking more closely at the two primary functions, we see that included in each of them are several roles that the leader can exhibit. Each of these roles falls into either a content or a process function. First we will discuss the roles that come under content functions. There are five primary content roles: teacher, synthesizer, clarifier, timekeeper, and evaluator.

The first role we discuss is the **teacher.** As teacher, you will be giving information, presenting concepts, models and theories, and seeking information. Your primary task is to **communicate most effectively the material you want to cover.** It is important that you are clear and concise in your presentation, that it is stated simply, and is easy to follow. The heart of the workshop is the material to be presented. Therefore, the role of teacher is a critical content function.

The second role is **synthesizer.** The synthesizer's task is to **abstract important information and condense it for the participants.** As a leader, you are often summarizing the essence of a complex idea and translating it into a more simplified one. You may say for instance, "The essence of what has just been discussed is as follows," or "the implication of such an approach would be. . . ." Your major job then is to compress, condense, and simplify information, in other words, to synthesize.

The third role in the category of content functions is the **clarifier.** Undoubtedly there will be instances in the workshop when material that you present, or that someone else presents, will be unclear. As clarifier, you need to **give examples and elaborate further on a thought or an idea that may be confusing to participants.** Or, you may need to re-word another person's statement in order to convey the message in a clearer way.

The fourth function is that of **timekeeper.** As timekeeper you must **make sure that enough time is allotted for each part of the design.** It is easy to get carried away, sidetracked, or become extremely involved so that you lose track of the time. Therefore, it is important to keep close to your time limits, remembering their importance, while allowing yourself some flexibility. Monitor discussions to be sure they fit into the time frame for particular segments of the workshop. For example, you may say to participants, "Spend thirty minutes practicing this skill in small groups. Then we will gather together and discuss how things went for about fifteen minutes." Or you might say, "Let's discuss this point for another five minutes. Is there anything you would like to add that has not been mentioned so far?" Thus you can remind participants of the time constraints, while helping them bring to closure the task at hand.

The final role in this category is that of **evaluator.** The evaluator's task is to **assess the progress that has been made towards the goal, as well as the participants' reactions to the material.** You are helping group members identify how far they have progressed in terms of reaching the goals, and what still remains to be completed before the workshop is over. For example, you may say, "So far we have covered and learned the following material. What we still need to cover is . . ." This type of leadership intervention helps participants to organize their experience in terms of accomplishments and in terms of what still remains to be learned and integrated. As an evaluator, you also need to ask for the group's reactions to the workshop. Thus, not only are you pointing out to participants where they are in terms of meeting the objectives of the workshop, you are also learning to what extent the workshop is meeting the needs of the participants.

Process Functions

As previously stated, process interventions are those statements or questions made by the leader that relate to the interactions, behaviors, or feelings of the participants. Although people generally come to workshops in order to learn new material, the way they feel as they learn will play an important part in how they conceptualize the workshop experience. There are five roles that relate to process functions. They are: facilitator, mediator, climate-setter, pulse-taker, and encourager.

The first role is that of **facilitator.** The facilitator must **make sure that all participants who wish to speak get heard.** You encourage others to express their points of view, their feelings, or thoughts. If you notice certain people are quiet, you might attempt to create an opening in the discussion for them to express their ideas or feelings. As facilitator you might say, "We have heard from several people, and there are still others who may want to add something."

The second role is that of **mediator.** The mediator helps **iron out any differences between members of the group.** At times group members may enter into controversies which impede the progress of the workshop. As leader, you would attempt to open up communication between those involved in the conflict, making sure that both parties are fully heard and understood. You might also suggest a new way to look at the issue under contention, which could then bridge the gap between the two dissenting sides.

The third role is that of **climate-setter.** In using the word climate, we mean **the atmosphere that is created by certain rules, procedures, norms, and behaviors set by the leader.** If there are specific behaviors you would like to see evidenced, you can demonstrate these behaviors yourself, so as to give others permission to behave similarly. For example, if you want participants to share their feelings as well as their ideas, you could encourage this behavior by expressing some of your feelings and experiences. Talking about your own personal experiences and feelings actively demonstrates your willingness to be open and self-disclosing. If you want certain rules to be followed during the workshop, such as no smoking, or no interrupting when someone is speaking, it is important to discuss these rules at the beginning. Of course, it is equally important that you follow these rules. In addition, you can encourage participants to influence the rules and procedures of the workshop by asking them to decide what rules and behaviors they would like to see exhibited. By encouraging participants to actively create the best climate in which they can learn, you are paying attention to their personal needs and feelings. You can influence whatever atmosphere you would like to see established. Your verbal and non-verbal behavior will support the kind of climate you would like to set.

The fourth process function is that of **pulse-taker.** By the word pulse, we mean the "feeling tone" of the group. **Periodically, you need to determine how people are feeling and how they are reacting to the workshop.** By taking the pulse of the group you can determine whether or not you need to make any changes in the design. For example, you might summarize how you perceive the group members are feeling, and then ask them to concur or to add a different perception. Taking the pulse of the group can mean conducting a mini-evaluation. For example, you might ask participants to describe in one sentence, their reactions to being in the workshop. Or, you might ask people to take a moment to express how they are feeling in general.

People like to feel responded to and cared about. Taking the pulse of the group is an important way to demonstrate concern for the participants' feelings and needs.

The fifth and last role we identify in this section is that of **encourager.** An encourager should **be warm, friendly, and responsive.** It is important to create a climate conducive to learning, risk-taking, and experimenting with new skills. Being encouraging helps to promote these behaviors. As an encourager you can state and practice the dictum, **"If something is worth doing, it is worth doing badly at first."** By supporting the ideas of participants, by taking risks yourself, by allowing enough time for practice and a lot of room for error, you are exhibiting encouraging behavior. People learn best in a friendly, supportive climate. Therefore, encouraging participation and experimentation is an essential role for building and strengthening a group.

To be an effective group leader you need to be able to intervene on both the content and the process levels of the group. It is therefore essential that you understand not only these two functions, but also the various roles that fall under each of them. Familiarize yourself with the kinds of leadership behaviors that relate to these roles, and practice the behaviors whenever possible.

MANAGING DIFFICULT BEHAVIORS

In this section we identify some negative behavioral patterns that are occasionally manifested by group members and that cause difficulty for group leaders. We have labelled these patterns in order to help you identify them. In doing so, we provide clues and examples which should help you to recognize people who might be difficult to deal with. Finally, we provide some suggestions about ways you might respond in order to minimize the negative behavior. Some of the suggestions are more direct than others. We encourage you to choose the one that seems most comfortable to you, or even better, to develop your own responses that will help reduce the negativity.

It is important to keep in mind that one or two responses, though they may be perfect examples of a pattern we are describing, do not make a pattern. In other words, it is not necessary or appropriate to intervene each time a group member manifests a disruptive bit of behavior. Only when this behavior becomes repetitive, is having a negative effect on the group, or is becoming irritating to you, does it

Difficult Behaviors

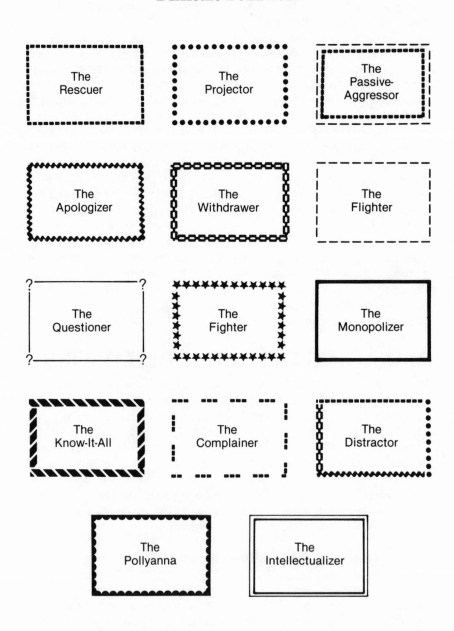

The Rescuer

The Projector

The Passive-Aggressor

The Apologizer

The Withdrawer

The Flighter

The Questioner

The Fighter

The Monopolizer

The Know-It-All

The Complainer

The Distractor

The Pollyanna

The Intellectualizer

become a pattern. At that point it is desirable to intervene in order to eliminate the behavior. It is also important to keep in mind that people can and do change. If you must label someone's behavior, remember that **the behavior is not the person.** It is only one aspect of the person. When an individual is primarily showing a negative side, it is difficult to see the positive side. You, as leader, need to reinforce any positive behaviors and attempt to minimize the negative ones.

The Rescuer

People who exhibit this behavior tend to "make nice." They apologize, defend, interpret for others, and explain away their own and other people's feelings. They tend to get frustrated or frightened by conflict, and they protect others as a way of avoiding the conflict situation. They are easy to recognize because they preface statements with phrases like, "I think what she really meant was . . ." or "You shouldn't feel that way; what he really meant was . . ." or "You shouldn't say that to Sam because he may take it the wrong way . . ."

Group leaders often find themselves getting angry at rescuers. If they express this anger they may begin to wonder if they are coming on too strong or being too confrontative. If the group leader is uncomfortable with conflict, then it might take longer to recognize rescue behavior, as the leader might feel some relief when rescue attempts are made. Rescuers need to learn that conflict is okay, that it is possible to have conflict and still feel good about one another. The leader's interventions should be geared towards helping the rescuer feel more comfortable in the face of conflict.

> **INTERVENTION STRATEGIES: THE RESCUER**
> - When the rescuer is attempting to interpret for someone else, say, "I'm aware that you are speaking for Alice. What I suggest is that you let Alice speak for herself." Or,
> - "I would prefer that people speak for themselves. Communication gets bogged down when people interpret for others."
> - When the rescuer is trying to avoid conflict you can say, "You seemed uncomfortable when Joe got angry. Is that true?"

The Projector

The projector attributes his or her own thoughts and feelings to other people. Often projectors are unaware that it is they who are experiencing the feeling, probably because it is so uncomfortable for them. Different feelings can be unpleasant for different individuals. Some people are afraid of anger, others are afraid of sadness, and still others are afraid of fear. The feelings we tend to project onto others are the ones with which we are most uncomfortable. Occasionally, one or more members will seem to be continually projecting their feelings onto others. Projectors make statements like "I don't think anyone understands the material," or "People are angry that you are not going to cover . . .," or "Cheryl was upset when you talked about . . ."

Projectors, although they appear to be speaking for other people, are actually speaking for themselves. You can recognize them because they either talk in generalities or talk about other people. They rarely make statements for themselves. You also begin to get an uncanny sense that the feeling they attribute to others is really their own. Sometimes projections are accurate, but it is important to remember that they are still projections. In other words, if John makes a statement about how Eric feels, and the statement actually reflects John's feelings, it may also be an accurate statement of Eric's feelings. That fact, however, does not mean you allow the projection to stand. Only if both John and Eric speak for themselves will you know how they each may feel.

INTERVENTION STRATEGIES: THE PROJECTOR
- "You've just made a statement for the group. Is that statement true for you?"
- "I'm wondering if that is really the way *you* feel."
- "Let's check out whether other people are really experiencing the feelings you are attributing to them."

The Passive-Aggressor

This kind of behavior can be difficult to notice at first, as it is indirect rather than direct. **Passive-aggressive people are hostile or angry but they express their hostility in subtle and indirect ways.** Often they attempt to mobilize group members to express the negative feelings they are experiencing. What usually occurs is that everyone begins to feel uncomfortable. Generally passive-aggressive people project their anger or uncertainty onto the leader, and the leader may begin to feel defensive. Participants exhibiting passive-aggressive behavior tend to do the following: come a little late to meetings and be mildly disruptive when they arrive, initiate occasional side conversations when someone else (generally the leader) is speaking, and maintain a somewhat unpleasant or disinterested facial expression. They often make mildly hurtful statements to people in the group, particularly the leader, but if confronted about their intentions they retreat and claim they did not mean anything negative by their remarks. They often make unpleasant statements within earshot of the person they intend to hurt. For example, a woman turned to another woman immediately after the first session of a workshop had ended and said just loud enough for the leader to hear, "I hope the next meeting will be more productive than this one." They seem to have a knack for sensing the leader's Achilles heel.

A group leader often feels defensive around passive-aggressive people. Or he or she may begin to feel like someone is "out to get him or her." These people tend to bait the leader, but they back off, act naive, and play the victim when the leader attempts to deal with them directly. The leader is often left feeling foolish and the behavior gets reinstated at a later point. In attempting to eliminate this kind of

---

**INTERVENTION STRATEGIES:
THE PASSIVE-AGGRESSOR**

- Take time for a general evaluation. You can say, "Let's take a minute to see how people are feeling about the workshop now." If the passive-aggressor responds negatively, thank him or her for the feedback. If he or she responds positively or says nothing, say "I'm glad you seem to be responding well to the workshop so far."
- If the individual makes a negative statement about the group and seems to be speaking for others, rephrase the statement so that it pertains only to the speaker. If John says "That last exercise was a waste of time," say "You feel, John, that the last exercise was a waste of time."
- If you feel a need to confront the person directly about his/her anger, and he/she is able to express it, then you have succeeded in cutting off the indirect passive-aggressive behavior. If the individual denies any angry or negative feelings, then simply say, "I'm sorry, I must have misread you. I'm glad everything is fine."

Leading the Workshop

behavior it is important that the leader does not get into an argument with the passive-aggressive person, and does not make an attempt to confront the behavior directly. The passive-aggressor, in retreating, believes he or she has "gotten" the leader, and the leader will then feel "had." It is tempting to want to please a person who you feel is responding negatively, but it is important not to, because then he or she will have received extra attention that will only reinforce the behavior. Actually, it is best to be patient, to hope that another (or other) group member will get annoyed and confront the passive-aggressor, so as to end the battle between group member and leader. If you feel you need to intervene, however, the following strategies may be helpful.

The Apologizer

Apologizers tend to preface their questions or statements with an apology. They often begin with the words "Maybe I should not say this, but . . ." or "Maybe you have already answered this question, but . . ." or "I'm sorry for taking up so much time, but . . ." Apologizers are not negative or unpleasant people. They can be draining however, and they generally use up a lot of air time in a group. Although they tend to speak a good deal, their apology often reflects a deep level of insecurity; underneath they usually feel very unsure of themselves.

Leaders often have mixed emotions towards apologizers. On the one hand, they may feel like protecting them or reassuring them. On the other hand, they may feel very annoyed at their repeated apologies. The group leader needs to encourage the person to assert himself or herself without any excuses, and to let the person know his or her comments or questions are valid. Ironically enough, the more confidence an apologizer gains, the less air time he/she will require.

INTERVENTION STRATEGIES: THE APOLOGIZER
- It is best to be direct with apologizers. You can say, "I feel badly that you apologize each time you speak. Your concerns are legitimate. There is no need to apologize for yourself."
- "You have made some very interesting points. You do not need to apologize for speaking."
- "Would you please ask your question again; this time experiment with omitting the apology."

The Fighter

People who exhibit fighting behavior in a group argue or disagree with most things that are said. They give the impression they want to pick a fight by asking questions or making comments in a provocative way. Their questions are really statements. They often begin by saying, "Don't you think that . . ." They are easy to recognize as their tone of voice is often belligerent. They seem to be continually looking for an argument. Usually fighters are struggling for power or control, and their questions or disagreements with the leader are the means by which they attempt to assume control. Individuals who are fighters are often people who feel quite powerless in their own lives and the struggle they exhibit in the group parallels their own personal struggles.

Group leaders generally feel furious with fighters. Fighters appear to be demonstrating how smart they are at the leader's expense. Sometimes a leader even begins to question his or her own knowledge and credibility. At times, he or she begins to experience some feelings of insecurity, which is, of course, what the fighter hopes will happen because then he or she can feel more powerful than the leader. It is important, as a leader, not to support the hostile part of the fighter. Support instead his or her knowledge and creative thinking.

INTERVENTION STRATEGIES: THE FIGHTER

- If the fighter is continually picking apart your statements or finding fault with the material, say, "It sounds like you have some interesting ideas. I'd really like to hear you elaborate on them."
- If the fighter says, "Don't you think that . . ." say, "It sounds like you have a statement to make. You are not really asking a question."
- You can confront the negativity by saying, "You sound irritated to me. Is there something bothering you?" If the fighter expresses some negative feelings, it is important to thank him or her for telling you and not to respond by getting into an argument about what was said.

The Flighter

This person seems to be in another world; **he or she often "tunes out," misses directions, or just does not seem to grasp the**

material. Often flighters "play dumb" rather than admit their attention is elsewhere. They are annoying in groups because they ask leaders to repeat directions or points everyone else understood. Their investment in the group seems low. When asked for an opinion they often respond by saying, "I don't care," or "Whatever you want," or "It makes no difference to me." During the workshop they often have blank expressions on their faces. Flighters can be annoying to leaders because t heir emotional involvement is usually minimal. When they do seem involved, it is often in order to ask the leader to repeat what he or she said. It is difficult to get angry at flighters because they tend to be soft spoken or apologetic when they are asking for clarification, or they are very agreeable when it comes to making decisions. It is important, as a group leader, not to reinforce "playing dumb" and to encourage flighters to assume responsibility for their behavior, otherwise their behavior will continue. They can be confronted directly.

INTERVENTION STRATEGIES: THE FLIGHTER
- If a flighter asks you to repeat material that you believe was quite clear, ask him or her to repeat first what he or she *did hear. You can then ask other group members to fill in the rest.*
- If you notice the flighter getting distracted you can say, "You seem to be distracted right now. Is there something on your mind?"
- If they are "playing dumb" ask them to guess at an answer, or to make one up if they have to.
- If they seem reluctant to give their opinion or to make a choice, get them to choose regardless. Say, "Even though you don't have much of a preference, please make a choice anyway."

The Questioner

The questioner can cause you difficulty because he or she is repeatedly stopping the flow of your presentation by asking questions. These questions may be about the content, the procedure, or about your style of leading the workshop. Questioners often ask a lot of "why" questions that you may begin to find difficult to answer and which can make you feel defensive. You will probably begin to feel irritated by these persistent interruptions. Often questioners have trouble thinking for themselves. Rather than finding their own answer to a thought or question, they will ask you to figure out the answer for them. It is important not to encourage this behavior. Instead, make some appropriate interventions that will enhance the development of this person's own problem solving skills. You will undoubtedly notice that you are not the only person irritated by the questioner's behavior. Other group members will find this continual questioning to be distracting and annoying as well. Asking repeated questions is usually a way to gain attention, though the attention received is often negative.

When relating to a person who asks a lot of questions you need to encourage this individual's thinking for himself or herself. Encourage the questioner to figure out some answers or to discuss the questions with other participants at a later time. Hopefully the questioner will then begin to feel more self-sufficient and confident about his or her problem-solving ability. As mentioned earlier, it is important not to gratify the questioner by answering each question. You will only encourage the behavior, feel more and more annoyed, and perhaps even "lose" other members.

INTERVENTION STRATEGIES: THE QUESTIONER

- "I appreciate your interest in the material and I think it would be helpful for you to experiment with answering that question yourself."
- "Take a guess as to what I meant by that statement."
- "We only have a limited amount of time. Would you save your question. It may be addressed later on."
- "Instead of answering that now, why don't you see me during the break if your question has not been answered by then."
- "What do you think the answer to that question is?" If the questioner responds by saying he or she does not know, say, "Take your time. When you get an idea let us know."

The Withdrawer

The withdrawer sits quietly in the group but looks miserable. He or she calls attention to himself or herself by looking pained, blank, or even disgusted. The group is generally aware of the feelings of this person even though he or she is being quiet. The withdrawer's facial expression clearly communicates displeasure, but the rest of the body gestures are quite still and withdrawn. Other members of the group generally feel awkward when they notice this person's quiet but obvious discomfort. If participants attempt to ignore this person's behavior there is usually a feeling of increased awkwardness.

The withdrawer needs to be encouraged to verbally express the non-verbal messages he or she is so strongly communicating. Generally, the withdrawn person is not fully aware of the impact he or she is having on the group. Therefore, it is important to address this type of behavior in a non-critical way. You need to provide an opportunity for the expression of negative feelings, and to create an atmosphere where it is safe to do so. Reaching out to a withdrawn person often affects his or her behavior in a desirable way. Continual reaching out without receiving a response, however, will only make you feel frustrated. It is possible that even if you encourage the expression of negative feelings, a withdrawn person will deny any dissatisfaction with the workshop experience. In this case it is best to say something like, "I am glad everything is all right. I must have misread you." If you continue your attempts to draw out the withdrawer, you may then find yourself getting angry, which is probably the exact response he or she hoped would occur.

If the withdrawer's behavior continues and seems to be having a disruptive effect on the group, you might decide to talk to the individual privately during a break, in which case it is important to attempt to determine if his or her dissatisfaction is due to the workshop itself, the dynamics of the group, a personal issue, or just a general attitude. Let the person know how this behavior is affecting you.

INTERVENTION STRATEGIES: THE WITHDRAWER
- "Is there something about what we are doing that is not of interest to you?"
- "I've been aware of what seems to be a pained look on your face for most of the morning. Perhaps you would like to tell us what you are feeling."
- "Susan, why don't you take this opportunity, while we are evaluating this segment of the workshop, to express your feelings and thoughts; you seem to be displeased."
- "I encourage you to express your point of view. Perhaps you can influence what we are currently doing."

The Monopolizer
The monopolizer takes up a great amount of "air time" in a workshop. As a result, sometimes participants begin to withdraw rather than fight for time to speak. The monopolizer is generally a poor

listener who usually manages to turn the conversation back to himself or herself. People exhibiting this behavior are often long winded and tend to interrupt others in order to state a personal opinion or relate an experience. This person seems unaware that there are others who might want to speak. Almost always when there is a pause in the conversation, he or she jumps right in, attempting to relate personally to the topic. As the leader you may find yourself praying that someone will beat them to the next opening in the conversation. Some group members may fight for air time, others may just give up, feeling there is no use struggling.

Your strategy with monopolizers needs to be encouraging. Invite them to practice an alternative behavior such as active listening. Do not attempt to completely stop the monopolizer from talking. Rather, attempt to limit the constant participation by encouraging the monopolizer to listen attentively to others and to be receptive to new ideas.

If confronted too directly, the monopolizer may feel hurt. Therefore, choose language that is supportive rather than critical in order to provide motivation for a behavioral change. You can make your intervention indirectly to the group, or more directly to the individual. It is probably best to make statements first to the group as a whole. If the monopolizer's behavior does not change, then it is necessary to address him or her directly. Usually an intervention addressed to the whole group gets the point across without causing unnecessary embarrassment.

INTERVENTION STRATEGIES: THE MONOPOLIZER
- "We have been primarily hearing from one or two people. I'm interested in hearing from the rest of you."
- "It might be helpful for those of you who have been doing a lot of talking, to listen more and for those of you who have been doing a lot of listening, to try speaking up more often."
- "Notice your style of participating. Have you been primarily a listener or a talker in this workshop? Practice exhibiting the opposite behavior and see what new things you can learn."
- "You have made some interesting comments and now I would like you to give some other people an opportunity to speak."

Leading the Workshop

The Know-It-All

The know-it-all is the person who is the expert on everything.
Regardless of what you say, he or she either adds something or corrects what you have said. Know-it-alls have ideas about almost everything and are very quick to offer their opinions, whether they are solicited or not. They want to feel important and show they are knowledgeable. Therefore, know-it-alls attempt to get recognition and power by taking the role of the resident expert.

When working with know-it-alls it is important to communicate that you know what they are doing. You can bring their behavior to their attention while suggesting that they can learn from other people. A know-it-all is actually attempting to discredit the leader by getting into an argument with him or her, and by winning the argument. Therefore it is important not to get into an argument with the know-it-all. A disagreement will take up an enormous amount of time and energy, and you, as leader, will probably find yourself in a battle of wits. With someone who is exhibiting know-it-all behavior, there is actually no way that he or she can win. If the know-it-all feels he or she has discredited you, it will then be hard for him or her to learn anything from you, as it is difficult to learn from someone you have just discredited. Therefore, it is essential for both of you not to get entangled in any discussions that promote a winner or a loser. You need to create a situation in which you both can win, where neither you nor the participant are discredited.

INTERVENTION STRATEGIES: THE KNOW-IT-ALL

- ''It seems that you have opinions on many subjects that are very different from mine. Would you like to come to the front of the room and present an opposing point of view?''
- ''You seem to know a lot about the subject. I'm wondering why you took this workshop.''
- ''Perhaps you would like to prepare a presentation and give it this afternoon, since you seem to have so many opinions on the subject.''
- ''Thank you for the information.'' Or, ''Thank you for your point of view.''
- ''You and I see the situation very differently. Although you certainly don't have to change your mind, I suggest that you let yourself be open to these new ideas. Let me know at the end of the workshop how you feel.''

The Complainer

The complainer continually finds fault with all aspects of the workshop. His or her criticism can include everything from dissatisfaction with the environment to dissatisfaction with the material being presented, to dissatisfaction with the structure. Therefore, you are likely to hear complaints like the following: "The seats are uncomfortable," "This workshop is not what I expected," or "I hate role playing." Complainers begrudgingly participate while letting you and everyone else know how they feel. Their feelings are not directly expressed; rather, they tend to moan and groan and make facial grimaces. As leader, you often hear them utter the words, "Do we have to?" This person tends to be a general "pain in the neck," and you may find yourself wishing he or she will not return after lunch. The complainer can take the fun out of leading a workshop. Therefore, it is important to ignore this type of behavior as much as possible and not take it too seriously, unless of course, several people are complaining about the same thing. The complainer intends for you to hear the snide remarks and to see the facial grimaces he or she makes. Try not to focus your attention on the complaints you overhear. Give your attention instead to those people who respond positively and directly. If it is not possible to tune out the moans and groans, and you feel you need to intervene, let your interventions to the complainer focus on how he or she can become more comfortable and satisfied. Do not try to take responsibility for their complaints, as they will only manufacture additional ones.

INTERVENTION STRATEGIES: THE COMPLAINER

- "You seem quite dissatisfied with most of the material being presented. What I hope is you will let yourself be open to it and reserve judgment until the end of the workshop. At the end of the workshop I would appreciate your feedback."
- "Even though I know you are not getting what you want right now, would you be willing to be receptive to what is being offered, and then decide later on how useful the material is to you?"
- "If nothing pleases you, perhaps you really do not want to be here."

The Distractor

The distractor often asks questions or makes comments that have nothing to do with the material currently being discussed.

Distractors change the topic by bringing up extraneous material, but they are usually unaware they are doing so. Their questions and comments divert attention from what is being discussed. These irrelevant comments often cause discomfort, as well as annoyance to the leader and to the participants. Responding to the comments and questions means getting sidetracked. It is difficult not to respond, however, because distractors are usually enthusiastic participants who do not consciously intend to cause trouble.

Sometimes these individuals experience uncomfortable feelings or thoughts generated by the material you are presenting. Changing the subject by making irrelevant comments can be an unconscious way of avoiding their unpleasant feelings. At other times, distractors are just not grasping the material. In these instances, it is possible that the material is too technical or too complicated for them to understand. When dealing with distractors it is helpful, through your interventions, to tell them what you observe is happening. You need to let them know, as gently as possible, that their questions are not appropriate at the time they are asking them.

INTERVENTION STRATEGIES: THE DISTRACTOR

- "That question does not seem to fit with what we are discussing right now. If it continues to seem important to you why don't you talk to me during the break."
- "You seem to be asking a lot of questions that are only slightly related to the topic we are discussing. Are you having difficulty understanding the material?"
- If people are raising their hands before speaking, you can avoid calling on the person exhibiting irrelevant behavior. If, however, participants are speaking without raising their hands you can say "Gee, Joe, we have heard from you a lot; let's hear some other points of view now."

The Pollyanna

A Pollyanna can initially be a delight to have in a group. This individual is always smiling, and his or her attitude is that everything is always wonderful and satisfying. Pollyannas rarely if ever express a preference or make a critical comment. They almost always go along with what the leader says or what the majority of the group wants. Nothing is ever a problem for them. **A Pollyanna will avoid conflict or disharmony at any cost.** She or he refuses to engage in any activity that might cause discomfort. A Pollyanna seems determined not to make waves, as the cost (experiencing negative feelings) might be too great. He or she attempts to smooth over or dismiss any negative feelings expressed by other group members, as these negative feelings might cause him or her to feel threatened or uncomfortable.

On the surface, it is wonderful to have a Pollyanna in a workshop because he or she will not cause any apparent trouble. After a while, however, the agreeable behavior begins to assume an unreal and annoying quality. You may begin to not trust the reactions of this person, since it is difficult to imagine everything is always as wonderful as he or she says. You may even start to wonder whether this individual is grasping the material. A Pollyanna's behavior is not at all desirable when group members are attempting to make a decision based on individual preferences. Trying to uncover a personal preference with a Pollyanna can seem nearly impossible.

When dealing with people who evidence Pollyanna behavior, your interventions need to be firm yet supportive. Gently insist the individual either make a choice or make a critical comment, depending on the situation. Support any indication of his or her expression of individuality. Where the Pollyanna does express a personal preference, provide verbal reinforcement. Support any risk-taking behavior that demonstrates he or she is in fact an individual with likes *and* dislikes.

INTERVENTION STRATEGIES: THE POLLYANNA
- If you are waiting for the Pollyanna to state a preference and he or she is avoiding responding, you can say, "Choose. Make a decision, any decision, as long as you decide."
- In an evaluation encourage him or her to give negative feedback as well as positive feedback. Say, "I really appreciate all your positive comments though I am sure the workshop was not 100 percent excellent. Find something you would like to see improved upon. It's important to give negative as well as positive feedback."
- "It is really nice to hear you give both positive and negative feedback."

The Intellectualizer
Intellectualizers tend to be quite verbose, and provide a lot of explanations for why they think or feel a certain way. **An intellectualizer at-**

tempts to make sense out of everything. When speaking, he or she uses many rationalizations and justifications for his or her beliefs. This person often becomes lost in his or her own theory. One way to recognize intellectualizers is by the way they often translate a very simple thought or idea into a complex theory. The more the intellectualizer talks, the more complicated a simple thought becomes.

You, as a leader, may find yourself getting lost, confused, or bored as the intellectualizer speaks. Your interventions should focus on helping this person keep the expression of ideas short and simple. The longer the intellectualizer talks, the more a simple idea becomes confusing and complex.

INTERVENTION STRATEGIES: THE INTELLECTUALIZER
- "Try expressing that idea in one sentence."
- "I am glad you are interested in that idea, but I am getting confused with how you are developing it."
- "I am getting lost in all of your words; see if you can say what you want to say more concisely."
- "It appears to me you are making what has just been said more complicated than is necessary."

We have presented several different kinds of behaviors which, when repeatedly exhibited in a workshop, can become troublesome for the leader. Although we do not like to label people, we have found the labels to be helpful only in so far as they aid us in identifying behavioral patterns. Remember that most participants exhibit any one of these behaviors at various times. Difficulty usually occurs only when an individual appears to exhibit one of these behaviors consistently.

We have offered several intervention strategies from which you can choose. Select only those interventions with which you feel most comfortable and that seem most appropriate to the given situation. Actually, we encourage you to develop your own strategies for dealing with difficult situations. It is important to remember, however, that leading a workshop is primarily fun, interesting, and exciting. Difficult individuals are usually the exception rather than the rule. Knowing how to handle potentially difficult and disruptive behaviors will give you more confidence in your leadership, which in turn will add to a more enjoyable and meaningful learning experience for participants.

CO-LEADING

Co-leading a workshop is a very different experience from leading a workshop alone. Although there are both benefits and drawbacks to co-leading, for the most part we believe co-leading a workshop is a positive experience that whenever possible should be encouraged. **Co-leading means you share the responsibility for conducting the group,** which includes the joys as well as the frustrations. Sharing responsibility however, does not have to be equal. One of you may be an assistant, rather than a co-leader, or one of you may happen to make more interventions than the other. As co-leaders, you can be helpful and supportive to each other by giving feedback aimed at increasing your skill levels. You can also learn from each other by observing each other's leadership styles and manners of presentation. Another advantage of co-leading is that the amount as well as the nature of the dynamics in a given group is so great one person cannot possibly be aware of all that is happening. Two leaders, however, can hear and see much more than one. Perhaps the only drawback of co-leading is that the time needed for preparation and designing is greater, as two people's ideas and desires need to be accommodated. As in designing, we define three basic areas to which you must pay attention in order to maximize the effectiveness of the co-leading experience: **stylistic differences, feelings, and responsibilities.** We will discuss each of these areas in this section.

Stylistic Differences Between Co-Leaders

Differences in leadership styles are highly beneficial. **Co-leaders can complement each other** as long as they each respect one another's style of working in a group. It is best if you can each describe and discuss your leadership style so you can determine what to expect from each other. This discussion will help to eliminate surprises and will create an effective team approach to co-leading. Although we discuss particular styles in this section, we believe an ideal leader needs to vary his or her style. The ideal leader has a range of behaviors available, depending on what seems appropriate at a given moment in the group. Different leadership behaviors are necessary in different groups. Therefore it is best to be flexible and to maximize your repertoire of leadership behaviors.

Under the area of stylistic differences, we have identified five major styles of leadership behavior. These styles can vary considerably

Co-Leading the Workshop

Co-Leading the Workshop diagram:

CO-LEADING / Pay Attention to: branches into three main areas:

STYLISTIC DIFFERENCES
- Activity vs. Passivity
- Intensity vs. Lightness
- Directness vs. Indirectness
- High Energy vs. Quiet Energy
- High Self Disclosure vs. Low Self Disclosure

FEELINGS
- About Each Other
- About The Workshop

RESPONSIBILITIES
- Content
  - teaching
  - synthesizing
  - clarifying
  - timekeeping
  - evaluating
- Process
  - facilitating
  - mediating
  - climate setting
  - pulse taking
  - encouraging

depending on the leader and on the situation. The first area of leadership style we call **activity versus passivity.** Some leaders are generally more active than others. Active leaders usually take more initiative in terms of introducing topics for discussion, making more interventions, and sharing their perceptions more frequently. Leaders who are generally more passive tend to wait for the group to mention an idea or to bring up a particular topic. Their response is often to initiate only if the group fails to do so. They allow the group process to develop with minimal input from the leader.

There are benefits and drawbacks to each approach. More passive leaders often encourage participants to assume greater responsibility for the workshop experience. At times, however, participants may feel resentful of this style of leadership, and want the leader to exercise more control over the group. The dynamics of the group are sometimes more visible if the leader observes frequently and intervenes minimally. If the group process is not highly significant to your workshop, however, waiting to see how group members will respond to group issues can be a poor use of time.

Active leaders often do a lot of teaching and share a lot of information. Their pressure is strongly felt through their interventions and they highly influence the tone, feeling, and mood of the workshop. A drawback to this style of leadership is that participants can become too dependent on the active leader to solve problems, make decisions, and keep the group moving. Ideally, if you are not attached to one particular leadership style, you will be able to determine whether more active or more passive leadership is more appropriate.

Another way in which leadership style can vary is **intensity versus lightness.** By this term we mean that some leaders use humor as a way to make the material more exciting and interesting. Other leaders may feel that humor detracts from the sincerity of the workshop, and they tend to express themselves more seriously. The leader's personality is an important determinant in this aspect of leadership style. Of course, you cannot force yourself to be humorous, but you can support and encourage group members to participate in a light and humorous way. As discussed earlier in this text, learning can be fun. Laughter and lightness do not imply lack of seriousness. What is important is to encourage and support lightness when appropriate. It is crucial that humor not detract from the context of the workshop; it should be used to enhance the learning experience.

Leading the Workshop

A third way in which leadership style may vary is **directness versus indirectness.** By these terms we mean the kinds of interventions a leader chooses to make. He or she may choose to confront people directly about their behavior, or choose to make general statements on a group level. For example, if Joe seems to be monopolizing much of the conversation, a leader whose approach tends to be direct would probably say, "Joe, I'd appreciate it if you would let others speak." A leader whose style is more indirect might say, "Let's try to let everyone have a chance to speak." The advantage of being direct is that the individual in question knows you are speaking to him or her. He or she can then choose or not choose to change his or her behavior. The group member may or may not feel offended by your directness. The advantage of being indirect is that the focus of attention is not on any particular group member and no one feels put on the spot. On the other hand, the troublesome person can deny you are speaking to him or her and completely miss the intention of your intervention.

Leadership style can also vary in terms of energy levels—**high versus quiet energy.** We have previously defined energy as levels of motivation, excitement, and desire. Some people have high energy levels. Often their energy takes the form of great excitement. This excitement can be catching and participants can become highly motivated by your high energy. If high energy becomes frenetic energy, however, it can be quite distracting. Participants may begin to feel overwhelmed. Leaders whose energy is more quiet and contained often evidence less enthusiasm. Their energy may be quiet and sustained, or low and listless. Quiet, prolonged energy allows participants to be interested in the material for longer periods of time without feeling drained. Low energy often results in participants feeling bored and tired. High energy people tend to gesture and move frequently and have much vocal inflection. Quiet energy people usually speak infrequently and in a low volume. Their gestures and bodily movements are more self-contained.

The fifth and final stylistic difference is **high versus low self-disclosure.** Self-disclosure means the willingness to share one's personal experiences as well as feelings in a group. Some leaders are much more comfortable doing so than others. Leaders who are high self-disclosers maintain less distance between themselves and participants than do low self-disclosers. For example, a leader who is a high self-discloser might choose to involve himself or herself in an introductory exercise in which people choose partners with whom to share personal information. A low self-disclosing leader might choose not to be personally involved in the exercise. Although we believe there is no right or wrong in the area of self-disclosure, some amount of personal sharing, even if small, is important. Some self-disclosure by the leader helps to create a climate of trust between group members and leader. A leader, however, needs to feel comfortable when self-disclosing, and therefore, he or she must ultimately decide how much or how little personal sharing is comfortable for him or her. The leader's behavior in this area may change from group to group, depending on the participants and on the nature of the workshop.

Feelings Between Co-Leaders

The second area to consider in co-leading workshops is **feelings**—the kinds of feelings that develop when two people work closely together. It is inevitable that you will experience a multitude of different feelings during the course of the workshop, and that these feelings will be positive, negative, or neutral. The kinds of emotions you experience towards your co-leader may be related to the way in which he or she responds to the group dynamics. For example, you may think your co-leader is confronting negative behavior too directly, and you may begin to feel uncomfortable in the group. You may think he or she is presenting the material somewhat inaccurately, or it would be much clearer if you were presenting it. Or, you may feel some of the design is not relevant to the participants.

As co-leaders, it is important that you decide how to deal with the range of feelings that develop between you. Sometimes co-leaders decide to express them openly in front of the participants. Other co-leaders decide to work them out privately during a break or a lunch hour. Discussing feelings in front of group members can be a positive experience for the participants. They have an opportunity to observe leaders' role model openness and honesty. It may help them be more open as participants. A drawback is that it takes up group time for leaders to work out their feelings towards each other.

Occasionally, group members get resentful when the leaders express conflict. Many leaders believe expressing positive feelings is a fine idea, but expressing negative feelings makes group members feel insecure. The major problem with waiting until the break to speak with your co-leader is that if the feelings are quite intense, or if they have existed for an extended period of time, the group members may sense them anyway. The tension in the air will probably be apparent. It is essential that you, as co-leaders, agree before the workshop how you will work out your feelings towards each other.

Co-Leader Responsibilities

The third and final area to consider in co-leading workshops is **responsibility.** There are two kinds of responsibility group leaders need to share: **content** and **process.** Responsibility for content refers to responsibility for the subject matter. Thus, **responsibility for content function roles includes teaching, synthesizing, clarifying, timekeeping, and evaluating.** Each of these roles are discussed at length in the section on "Leadership Functions." It is important to decide prior to the workshop how you will each be responsible for these roles. You and your co-leader must also decide whether it is permissible to add to something your co-leader says or to offer another point of view. In addition, you must decide whether it is acceptable to disagree with your co-leader or to correct what you believe are inaccurate statements. Make sure you and your co-leader discuss these issues prior to the workshop.

Responsibility for the process refers to those ways in which you will share responsibility for facilitating the process functions. **Responsibility for process function roles includes facilitating, mediating, climate-setting, pulse-taking, and encouragment of participants.** Each of these roles are fully discussed in the section on "Leadership Functions." You need to decide, however, prior to the workshop, how you will each be responsible for those rules.

It is important to remember that both leaders are responsible for the smooth functioning of the workshop. In addition to deciding ahead of time how to intervene on a group process level, you also need to decide how much of the workshop time you are willing to devote to the group process. Will you respond to it frequently or infrequently? Your decision will undoubtedly vary according to the objectives of the workshop. If you are co-leading a Counseling Skills Workshop, you will most certainly want to pay a great deal of attention to the group process since an important focus in counseling is the relationship between the client and the counselor, i.e., the "process" of counseling. If, however, you are co-leading a Resumé Writing Workshop, it is rarely necessary to spend time dealing with the group's dynamics. Therefore, allow the objectives of the workshop to help guide you in determining how much time to devote to group process.

It takes time to work out with your co-leader the ways in which you will manage the three areas: stylistic differences, feelings, and responsibilities. You will generally find, though, the additional time is well worthwhile. There is probably no better way to develop your leadership skills than to co-lead a workshop with someone whose leadership ability you trust. You can grow and learn from each other and enjoy yourself in the process. Finally, we wish to add that the low points in a workshop are not nearly as low, and the high points feel even higher when they are shared.

APPENDICES:
checklists & forms

A. KEY ELEMENTS IN WORKSHOP DESIGN

I. Gathering Information about Participants

As fully as possible, know your audience. Consider the following areas:

- **A.** Knowledge of the subject
- **B.** Size of the group
- **C.** Gender, age, marital status, ethnicity
- **D.** Belief systems, social and political orientations
- **E.** Needs
- **F.** Voluntary versus mandatory
- **G.** Familiarity of the participants with each other

II. Fun

Learning does not have to be painful. Work at exciting the "child" that lives in all of us. More fun for you, as a trainer, as well as for participants, if your "child" is involved. Learning will be hindered if the attention of participants is limited.

III. Time

Know your limits in terms of realizing your goals. Consider the following questions:

- **A.** How much time are you allotted?
- **B.** Are you building-in breaks?
- **C.** Are you building-in time for reflecting and integrating?
- **D.** Are you taking into account slippage (what you may not anticipate can still happen)?

IV. Appropriate Sequencing

There should be a natural flow to your design. Allow yourself to be sensitive to what you have come up with; ask yourself:

- **A.** Does the design have a beginning, a middle, and an end?
- **B.** Does each part of the design naturally flow into the next part of the design?
- **C.** Have you followed the principles of sequencing?

V. Simplicity

Beginning designers often make their designs too complex. The design needs to be easy to understand for both you and the participants. If you have had to read it over several times yourself, it is probably not simple enough.

VI. Variety

People are touched on several levels. Not all people learn from or are motivated by the same means. If you can include an appeal to the emotional, intellectual, physical, and spiritual parts of self, there is a greater chance of fuller response from the participants. Although this is not always possible, strive for it.

VII. Sharing Your Expectations

Most people like to have a sense of what to expect—how their morning will go, the day, or the eight-week course. Since most people are coming to your workshop with expectations, it is better to know in the beginning so you can respond to their enquiries, ''Yes, I think that will be met,'' or, ''No, I had something else planned.'' Thus you share your expectations and find out theirs.

VIII. Climate-Setting

The atmosphere or setting is an essential component in planning your design. Consider the following:

  A. Size of physical space
  B. Furniture arrangement (are pieces moveable?)
  C. Comfort (chairs, mats, pillows)
  D. Lighting
  E. Temperature
  F. Ambience (conducive for exploring, safety, intimacy?)
  G. Availability (will you have to move locations if workshop is ongoing?)

IX. Pacing

We each have an inner clock; no two persons' clocks are the same, though they may be similar. Paying attention to your pacing and to the participants' pacing is important. People require time to absorb material and experiences. Consider the following:

  A. What is your rate of presentation (talking, exercises)—too fast, too slow?
  B. Are you packing-in too much, or are things lagging and do people seem bored?

X. Flexibility

If after completing your design if it does not "feel" right, trust your feelings and re-work the design. If while carrying out your workshop, significant learnings and/or events are happening, be flexible. Remember that some activities/experiences may take more time than others or have more impact than you may have imagined.

XI. Evaluation

Paying attention to the "energy levels" of the participants and yourself will help you evaluate the workshop while it is still in progress, and at its conclusion. You may make last-minute changes throughout the experience according to your ongoing evaluations. Concluding evaluations serve the dual purpose of giving the trainer feedback and helping participants integrate what they have learned.

    A. Ongoing evaluations
    B. Concluding evaluations

B. FIVE EASY STEPS TO DEVELOPING A DYNAMIC DESIGN

Step 1. Establishing and Listing Your Goals

Be specific. "A goal is an end one strives to attain." Goals can be both cognitive and emotional. Many people confuse goals and methods, so be sure your goal states the end result you wish to attain.

A. Ask yourself the following:
    1. What do you want to see happen?
    2. What do you want people to go away with?
B. Determine whether or not your goals can be met in the allotted time
C. In case time is inadequate, *prioritize* your goals and set reasonable time limits for each one
D. Organize your goals in terms of a logical flow

Step 2. Brainstorming Methods

Considering one goal at a time, "brainstorm" methods for meeting that goal.

A. Be creative—assume the sky is the limit
B. Exhaust all possible ideas
C. Take off on your own or on other peoples' ideas.

Step 3. Selecting Methods and Structures

When you have exhausted through brainstorming all possible ideas, it is time to select the one(s) to use.

A. Select methods that will best achieve your goals, while taking into consideration the elements of a good design
    1. Structured experiences
    2. Non-structured experiences
    3. Lecturettes
    4. Processing
    5. Discussion
B. Select the most appropriate structure by which to implement the methods you have chosen.
    1. Intrapersonal
    2. Interpersonal
    3. Small group

4. Intergroup

5. Whole group

Step 4. Assessing the Design

Once you have finished your design it is essential to evaluate it, both objectively and subjectively, using the following criteria:

    A. Determine whether your goals are clearly stated and whether the methods you have chosen meet the goals.

    B. Determine whether your design meets the requirements of "Elements of a Good Design"

    C. Determine whether or not the design "feels" good to you. Ask yourself:

        1. Am I comfortable with this design?

        2. Can I pull this off—is it "me"?

        3. Would I enjoy this design if I were a participant?

Step 5. Revising of the Design

If the answer to any of the questions in Step 4C is "no," you need to make some revisions in your design. After you have made the necessary revisions, again go through the evaluation process until you can honestly answer "yes" to each question. At that point you can consider your dynamic design complete.

C. WORKSHEET: YOUR DESIGN

Workshop Title _____

_____

_____

Workshop Goals _____
(prioritize)
_____

_____

_____

_____

_____

_____

_____

_____

_____

_____

_____

_____

Methods Brainstormed _____
(all ideas)
_____

_____

_____

_____

_____

_____

_____

_____

_____

_____

_____

Methods Selected _____

_____

_____

_____

_____

_____

_____

_____

Structures Selected _____

_____

_____

_____

_____

_____

_____

Design Assessment

Objective:
- Are goals clearly stated?
- Will methods chosen achieve goals?
- Do methods chosen meet requirements of ''Elements of Good Design''?

Subjective:
- Does design ''feel'' good to you?
- Are you comfortable with design?
- Is this design you? Can you pull it off?
- Would you enjoy this design if you were a participant?

Yes	No	Comments

Necessary Revisions _____

_____

_____

_____

_____

C. WORKSHEET: YOUR DESIGN

Workshop Title _____

_____

_____

**Workshop Goals
(prioritize)** _____

_____

_____

_____

_____

_____

_____

_____

_____

_____

**Methods Brainstormed
(all ideas)** _____

_____

_____

_____

_____

_____

_____

_____

_____

_____

_____

_____

Methods Selected _____

_____

_____

_____

_____

_____

_____

Structures Selected _____

_____

_____

_____

_____

_____

_____

Design Assessment

Objective:

- Are goals clearly stated?
- Will methods chosen achieve goals?
- Do methods chosen meet requirements of "Elements of Good Design"?

Subjective:

- Does design "feel" good to you?
- Are you comfortable with design?
- Is this design you? Can you pull it off?
- Would you enjoy this design if you were a participant?

Yes	No	Comments

Necessary Revisions _____

_____

_____

_____

_____

C. WORKSHEET: YOUR DESIGN

Workshop Title _____

_____

_____

_____

**Workshop Goals
(prioritize)** _____

_____

_____

_____

_____

_____

_____

_____

_____

_____

_____

**Methods Brainstormed
(all ideas)** _____

_____

_____

_____

_____

_____

_____

_____

_____

_____

_____

Methods Selected _____

_____

_____

_____

_____

_____

_____

Structures Selected _____

_____

_____

_____

_____

_____

_____

Design Assessment

Objective:
- Are goals clearly stated?
- Will methods chosen achieve goals?
- Do methods chosen meet requirements of "Elements of Good Design"?

Subjective:
- Does design "feel" good to you?
- Are you comfortable with design?
- Is this design you? Can you pull it off?
- Would you enjoy this design if you were a participant?

Yes	No	Comments

Necessary Revisions _____

_____

_____

_____

_____

C. WORKSHEET: YOUR DESIGN

Workshop Title
_____

_____

_____

**Workshop Goals
(prioritize)**
_____

_____

_____

_____

_____

_____

_____

_____

**Methods Brainstormed
(all ideas)**
_____

_____

_____

_____

_____

_____

_____

_____

Methods Selected _____

_____

_____

_____

_____

_____

_____

Structures Selected _____

_____

_____

_____

_____

_____

_____

Design Assessment

Objective:
- Are goals clearly stated?
- Will methods chosen achieve goals?
- Do methods chosen meet requirements of "Elements of Good Design"?

Subjective:
- Does design "feel" good to you?
- Are you comfortable with design?
- Is this design you? Can you pull it off?
- Would you enjoy this design if you were a participant?

Yes	No	Comments

Necessary Revisions _____

_____

_____

_____

_____

C. WORKSHEET: YOUR DESIGN

Workshop Title _____

_____

_____

**Workshop Goals
(prioritize)** _____

_____

_____

_____

_____

_____

_____

_____

_____

_____

**Methods Brainstormed
(all ideas)** _____

_____

_____

_____

_____

_____

_____

_____

_____

_____

_____

_____

Methods Selected
_____

_____

_____

_____

_____

_____

_____

_____

Structures Selected
_____

_____

_____

_____

_____

_____

_____

Design Assessment

Objective:
- Are goals clearly stated?
- Will methods chosen achieve goals?
- Do methods chosen meet requirements of "Elements of Good Design"?

Subjective:
- Does design "feel" good to you?
- Are you comfortable with design?
- Is this design you? Can you pull it off?
- Would you enjoy this design if you were a participant?

Yes	No	Comments

Necessary Revisions
_____

_____

_____

_____

_____

D. LEADER SELF-EVALUATION FORM

Rate yourself on the following qualities. Assign yourself a score between 1 and 10 that reflects the frequency with which you possess each quality: give yourself a score of 10 if you believe you possess the quality all the time; give yourself a score of 1 if you believe you never possess the quality.

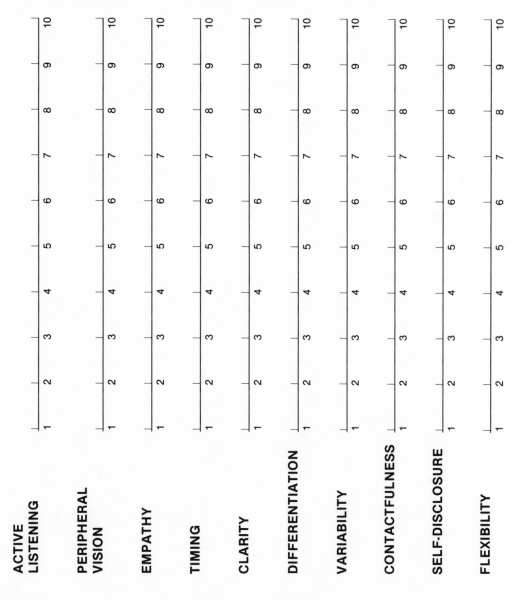

D. LEADER SELF-EVALUATION FORM

Rate yourself on the following qualities. Assign yourself a score between 1 and 10 that reflects the frequency with which you possess each quality: give yourself a score of 10 if you believe you possess the quality all the time; give yourself a score of 1 if you believe you never possess the quality.

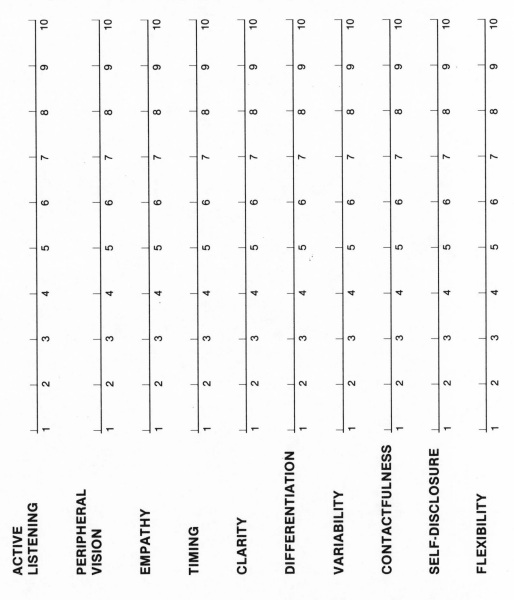

D. LEADER SELF-EVALUATION FORM

Rate yourself on the following qualities. Assign yourself a score between 1 and 10 that reflects the frequency with which you possess each quality: give yourself a score of 10 if you believe you possess the quality all the time; give yourself a score of 1 if you believe you never possess the quality.

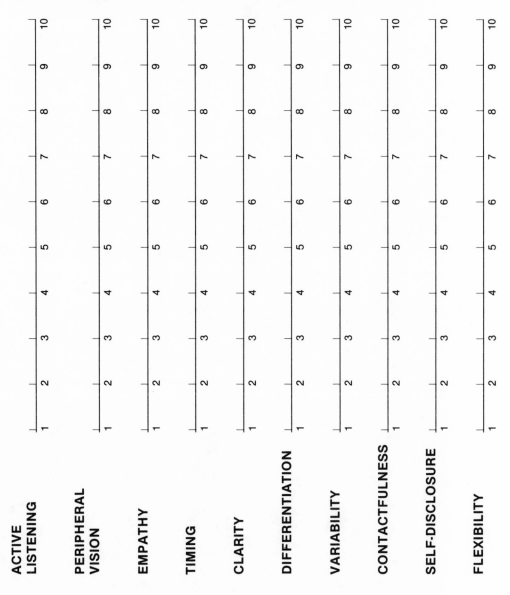

ACTIVE LISTENING

PERIPHERAL VISION

EMPATHY

TIMING

CLARITY

DIFFERENTIATION

VARIABILITY

CONTACTFULNESS

SELF-DISCLOSURE

FLEXIBILITY

D. LEADER SELF-EVALUATION FORM

Rate yourself on the following qualities. Assign yourself a score between 1 and 10 that reflects the frequency with which you possess each quality: give yourself a score of 10 if you believe you possess the quality all the time; give yourself a score of 1 if you believe you never possess the quality.

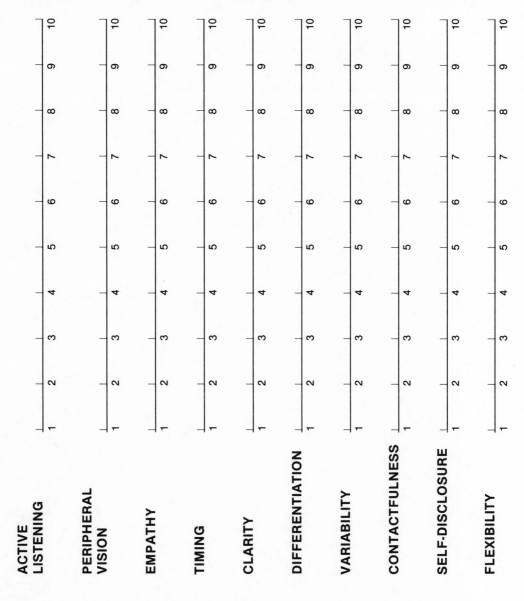

ACTIVE LISTENING

PERIPHERAL VISION

EMPATHY

TIMING

CLARITY

DIFFERENTIATION

VARIABILITY

CONTACTFULNESS

SELF-DISCLOSURE

FLEXIBILITY

D. LEADER SELF-EVALUATION FORM

Rate yourself on the following qualities. Assign yourself a score between 1 and 10 that reflects the frequency with which you possess each quality: give yourself a score of 10 if you believe you possess the quality all the time; give yourself a score of 1 if you believe you never possess the quality.

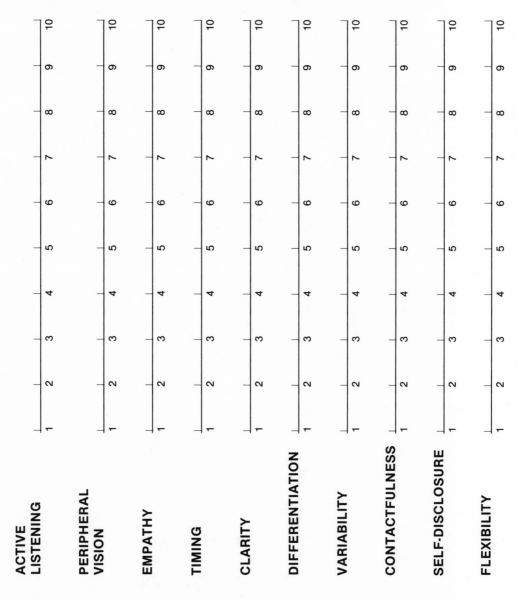

ACTIVE LISTENING

PERIPHERAL VISION

EMPATHY

TIMING

CLARITY

DIFFERENTIATION

VARIABILITY

CONTACTFULNESS

SELF-DISCLOSURE

FLEXIBILITY

NOTES

NOTES

NOTES